MARGERY FORDE is a Queensland based playwright. She was commissioned to write *X-Stacy* for La Boite Theatre. As well as being published by Currency Press, *X-Stacy* is published by Dramatic Lines, London. Margery has received the Trust Award for Excellence for Outstanding Contribution to Theatre in Queensland and Australia and the Playlab Award for Services to New Work in Queensland. Margery also received the Centenary Medal for Services to Queensland Theatre. She won the NSW Premier's Literary Award for Best Stage Play for *Milo's Wake* co-written with her partner Michael (La Boite). *Milo's Wake* is published by Currency Press. It also won the Matilda Award, the Perform/4MBS Award and received an AWGIE nomination. *Milo's Wake* has toured nationally and internationally with productions in New Zealand, London and at the Edinburgh Festival. It also had a translated production in Tokyo (Kaze Theatre Company). With Michael, other productions for La Boite include *Still Standing*, *James and Johnno* and *Way Out West* (Published by Playlab Press, ABaf Award*)*. Margery has received AWGIE Awards for her plays *What Next?* and *Snapshots from Home* for QPAT. (Published by Playlab Press.) With Michael, Margery wrote *Cribbie* for 4MBS Classic Arts published by Playlab Press, *Skating on Sandgate Road* (ACU and Q150). For the Queensland Music Festival, Margery and Michael wrote the script and lyrics for *Behind the Cane* (AWGIE nomination 2012, published by Playlab Press). With Michael, Margery wrote the music theatre production *Heart of an Open Country* for the Queensland Music Festival (2013).

X-STACY

Margery Forde

with Teacher's Notes by Helen Radvan

Currency Press • Sydney

CURRENCY TEENAGE SERIES
First published in 1999
by Currency Press Pty Ltd,
PO Box 2287, Strawberry Hills, NSW, 2012, Australia
enquiries@currency.com.au; www.currency.com.au
in association with
La Boite Theatre, Brisbane

Reprinted 2000.

This revised edition published 2000

Reprinted 2001, 2003, 2004, 2007, 2009, 2013, 2016, 2021

Copyright © Margery Forde, 1999, © Helen Radvan, 1999, Teacher's Notes.

NATIONAL LIBRARY OF AUSTRALIA CIP DATA
Forde, Margery
      X-Stacy.
      ISBN 9780868196022
      I. Radvan, Helen. II. Title.
A822.3

Typeset by Erin Dewar for Currency Press.
Cover design by Sasha Middleton, ToadShow.

Currency Press acknowledges the Traditional Owners of the Country on which we live and work. We pay our respects to all Aboriginal and Torres Strait Islander Elders, past and present.

Contents

For Michael and Katy

X-Stacy was first produced by La Boite Theatre, Brisbane, on 16 July 1998, with the following cast:

FERGUS	Philip Cameron-Smith
ANNE	Sharonlee Martin
BEN	Matthew Passmore
ZOE	Inez Fainga'a
JENNA	Leah Pappin
STACY	Caitlin Hunter
FATHER PAUL	Philip Cameron-Smith

Director, Sue Rider
Design, Kate Stewart
Lighting, Andrew Meadows
Sound Design, Michael Bouwman
Dramaturg, Saffron Benner
Assistant Director, Fraser Corfield
Stage Manager, Tiffany Noack

CHARACTERS:

BEN, a young man (about 20)

ANNE, Ben's mother (early 40s)

STACY, Ben's sister (we follow her journey from a 14-year-old to a 17-year-old)

FERGUS, DJ and friend of Ben (early 20s)

FATHER PAUL, a young priest and friend of Anne

JENNA, Stacy's friend and Fergus' girlfriend (late teens)

ZOE, uni student and DJ from Cairns (late teens)

SCENE ONE

The stage has the melancholy feeling of an old disused warehouse. It is bleak and colourless. Empty water bottles and clip-seal bags are scattered about the floor. As the audience enters, the cleaner is sweeping up the bottles and collecting them in garbage bags.

Lights go down. Into the beginnings of a haunting Gregorian chant. It continues throughout the following.

JENNA: (*answer machine*) Hi, this is Jenna. I can't come to the phone. Please leave a message. Thanks.

    A beep.

BEN: Jenna. It's Ben. Have you seen Stacy? Call me back.

    A pool of light slowly fades up on ANNE. *She is at mass. She stands facing the young priest,* FATHER PAUL, *on the altar.*

PRIEST:… and during the coming week, may your God go with you, brother, companion and comforter. Our Eucharist is ended. Let us go in peace to love and serve the Lord.

ANNE: Thanks be to God.

    The light fades down on ANNE. *The Gregorian chant bleeds into a 'doof'. DJ* FERGUS *weaves the spell to create the Crystal. Perhaps* FERGUS *is speaking with the voice-over of his own recorded voice.*

FERGUS: As you start to spin you feel this incredible surge of power. Doof! Doof! Doof! Doof! Like a heartbeat. You can feel it before you hear it. Doof! Doof! Doof! Doof! The power's there in the lights and the turntables… the speakers and the music. The perfect sounds build and build until they explode with pure energy. You are one tribe, one heartbeat. Put yourself in his hands, and the DJ will take you on a journey, to somewhere you've never been before, to a new world… just because of what he's spinning. He is in absolute control.

Full lighting effects up, the music explodes. We are in The Crystal, a dance party club. DJ FERGUS *is spinning his tracks at his mixing desk like a manic conductor. It's as if the dancers are worshipping at the altar of the high priest. Some carry luminous sticks of light or strobe torches. They are carried by the music into a state of ecstasy. Waves of screams, whistles and cheering as the music surges to new and more exciting peaks.*

A track of music with various highs and lows, and the way the dancers respond to them, their fluctuating energy levels, suggest that time is passing.

BEN *holds a water bottle as he dances. Also dancing are* ZOE *and* JENNA. *They are not dancing together… each is completely lost in his or her own world. The feeling is blissful, tribal, trance-like.*

Slowly the light focuses in on BEN *until he is left alone in his pool of light. A ghostly theme weaves into the music ('Stacy's Theme'). The light becomes more eerie. A girl,* STACY, *joins* BEN *in his pool of light.* STACY *and* BEN *do not dance together, but the feeling is that they are in some way united. Perhaps they mirror each other's movements.*

Music continues for a moment longer and then begins to slowly fade away. Lights come up. BEN *stands alone.* STACY *is gone.* BEN *is coming out of a trance-like state. There are cheers and whistles as the music ends. DJ* FERGUS *winds up the dance party.*

FERGUS: Thanks for coming. You guys were fucking wicked.

More cheers. BEN *has been dancing for hours. He looks at his watch.*

BEN: God.

He takes a drink from his water bottle and goes to put it in his backpack. He then approaches the DJ stand to help FERGUS *who is beginning to pack up. They are packing* FERGUS*'s collection of records, vinyls and CD's, into record boxes.*

FERGUS: So, how was it?

BEN: Goin' off man. Insane stuff.
FERGUS: Loony tunes.
BEN: Yeah, that was a hell of a cool set. Fantastic.
FERGUS: You've got to build a night, you know? Create a mood. Hardly anyone does that anymore. I'm trying a bit more scratching, did you notice?
BEN: Nuh. (*He laughs.*) Yeah, it was bloody brilliant. It was a great night.
FERGUS: Except I had this one guy front up and ask for a request.
BEN: You're kidding.
FERGUS: I said, if you want a jukebox, you'll have to shove a dollar up my arse.

BEN *laughs.*

Hey, I've been asked to guest at Revelation in Sydney next month, did I tell you?
BEN: No. Hey congratulations man. That party's gonna be huge.
FERGUS: Yeah. We are talkin' big time. Stay tuned.

JENNA *approaches.*

JENNA: Hi guys.
FERGUS: Hey look out. Stranger danger.

BEN *is shocked to see* JENNA.

JENNA: Hi Ben. How's it goin'?

BEN *ignores her and continues to pack.*

It's been a while, eh? How's your mum?

BEN *picks up a box of records and begins to carry them out to* FERGUS' *van.* JENNA *watches him go.*

FERGUS: Shit, Jenn. Not a good move, babe.
JENNA: I wanted to say hey, that's all.
FERGUS: I thought we decided you wouldn't come here tonight. Didn't I say that?
JENNA: I just wanted to see how he was doing.
FERGUS: I already told you, he's doing okay. But you just turning up out of the blue like this isn't going to help him.
JENNA: I've had nine months of thinking about it Fergus.

FERGUS: And he's had nine months to get over it.
JENNA: You said you were coming to Sydney.
FERGUS: I was coming.
JENNA: Yeah, fucking so's Christmas.

> JENNA *begins to leave.* FERGUS *goes to her and puts his arms around her. They cling to each other in silence for a moment.*

FERGUS: You okay?
JENNA: I guess.
FERGUS: You been here long?
JENNA: Long enough to catch some of your set.
FERGUS: What did you think?
JENNA: It was alright.
FERGUS: Eh?
JENNA: You tore the place up, man. You're still the best.

> BEN *enters and picks up another box and exits to* FERGUS' *van.* JENNA *watches him.*

FERGUS: And you're still too thin. Are you eating?
JENNA: Yes.
FERGUS: You've got to eat, Jenn.
JENNA: No shit, Fergus.
FERGUS: Listen, I've got a few things to finish off here, some packing and stuff. You go and get yourself some breakfast. There's that place just up the street.
JENNA: I'm not hungry.

> FERGUS *takes out his wallet and hands* JENNA *some cash.*

FERGUS: I'll meet you there soon, okay? Then we can go home.
JENNA: Don't be long.

> JENNA *begins to exit as* BEN *re-enters with* FERGUS' *van keys.*

'Bye Ben.

> JENNA *exits.* BEN *watches her go.*

FERGUS: She lobbed up on my doorstep this afternoon.
BEN: Where'd she disappear to?
FERGUS: Sydney.
BEN: Yeah, that'd be right.

Momentary pause.

FERGUS: She's staying with me for a while.

BEN *looks at* FERGUS *in disbelief.*

BEN: What?

FERGUS: What could I do? She's got nowhere else. Hey, you saw her, man. She looks bad.

BEN: I don't give a shit.

FERGUS: Ben, come on, man…

BEN: No. Bullshit, Fergus.

FERGUS: What was I supposed to do? Leave her out on the street?

BEN: Fine. Look, you do whatever you want. Just tell her to stay right away from me.

FERGUS: I already told her.

BEN: Well, tell her again. Fuck.

FERGUS: Ben, it's all right.

BEN: No. No it's not all right.

FERGUS: I'll have another talk to her. Just take it easy, huh?

BEN: (*mimicking*) Huh?

FERGUS: I wasn't expecting this either, you know? Come on, man. Would I do this to you?

BEN: Yeah.

They laugh. The tension is broken. FERGUS *moves to a box at the DJ desk.*

FERGUS: Hey, I was wondering if you could do me a favour.

BEN: Here we go.

FERGUS *takes a flyer from the box and hands one to* BEN. BEN *scans it.*

FERGUS: Flyers for the rave.

BEN: (*reading*) A Rave New World…

FERGUS: You like?

BEN: I like. So where's it going to be happenin'?

FERGUS: Ah, only Fergus knows. But all will be revealed in the fullness of time.

BEN: Cool.

FERGUS: Spread 'em around. Might be worth some freebies.

BEN: Yeah, this looks pretty damn fine.

FERGUS: It's gonna be a gathering of souls, man.

> ZOE *approaches. She is preparing to leave the club. She is wearing her backpack and carrying a bottle of water.*

ZOE: Hi.

BEN: Hi.

ZOE: (*to* FERGUS) I enjoyed your set. It was choice.

FERGUS: Thank you. We do our best.

ZOE: I'm Zoe.

FERGUS: Fergus.

ZOE: Yeah. That stuff you were spinning. Far out, man.

FERGUS: Thanks. This is Ben.

BEN: Good party?

ZOE: Yeah. Excellent. I've never been here before. I'm new to Brisbane… thought I'd suss out the scene.

FERGUS: Good move.

ZOE: So, you're resident DJ in this place?

FERGUS: Yep.

ZOE: Cool. I'm a DJ

FERGUS: Oh. Okay.

> FERGUS *exchanges a look with* BEN.

ZOE: I was hoping I might be able to get some gigs down here.

BEN: Listen, I gotta go.

FERGUS: Alright man. Check you tomorrow huh?

BEN: Yep.

> BEN *picks up the box of fliers.*

FERGUS: Thanks for your help. And look, I'm sorry about that before.

BEN: It's okay. I'll see ya. (*To* ZOE) 'Bye.

ZOE: See ya.

> BEN *exits.*

Yeah, I did some DJ-ing back home in Cairns. It took me ages, but I saved up enough cash to buy a mixer and some amps and some speakers and stuff.

FERGUS: Expensive hobby.

ZOE: It's not a hobby. I had a regular gig up there.

FERGUS: Oh. Sorry.

ZOE has positioned herself behind the turntables and is pretending to play.

ZOE: I used to get a great response from the crowd too. You have to know how to program a set, don't you… to play just the right thing at the right moment.

FERGUS: It helps.

ZOE: You play a sucker of a track, you lose 'em.

FERGUS: Hey watch it!

FERGUS *moves* ZOE *away.*

ZOE: You have to play *to* a crowd and not *for* a crowd.

FERGUS: Absolutely.

ZOE: I wouldn't want a full time gig. Just part time. I'm at uni.

FERGUS: How's it going?

ZOE: Oh, you know.

FERGUS: Excellent. Well, I'd better get the rest of my shit organised. Great talking to you… uhm…

ZOE: Zoe.

FERGUS: Right.

FERGUS *begins to move in the direction of the DJ platform.*

ZOE: Hey, hold on a tick.

ZOE *rifles in her backpack and produces a tape. She hands it to* FERGUS.

It was recorded at one of my gigs. It gives you an idea of the kind of stuff I do.

ZOE *points to her name on the label.*

That's my DJ name.

FERGUS: Zo-E.

He pretends not to get the play on the name. Then as if it has just dawned on him…

Oh. Zo-E. Zoe. Hey!

FERGUS *hands the tape back to her.*

ZOE: Oh no, keep it. You might like to have a listen sometime.

FERGUS *puts the tape in his pocket.*

I'm really interested in experimental stuff. I have all this music inside my head, you know? And I just want to share it with people.

FERGUS: That's great.

ZOE: Actually, I've just picked up a whole heap of amazing vinyls from Lifeline.

FERGUS: Funky.

ZOE: Thirty cents each, can you believe it?

FERGUS: Yeah.

ZOE: So, I suppose to crack it in the club scene down here you'd have to have a few connections.

FERGUS: Doesn't hurt.

ZOE: Thought so. I really don't know too many people yet.

FERGUS: Yeah well, better to get work because you're a good DJ, not because you know people in the industry, hey? Anyway, I've got some valuable gear sitting out in the van.

ZOE: Oh, sorry. I'd better let you go. Excellent party tonight, man.

FERGUS: Thanks. Come again.

ZOE: No worries. See ya.

FERGUS: Yeah. See ya.

ZOE *exits.* FERGUS *takes the tape out of his pocket and looks at it.*

FERGUS: Zo-E. Wannabe. Shit.

SCENE TWO

Voice over: BEN*'s phone call to* FERGUS.

FERGUS: (*with techno music in background*) Greetings earthlings. Sorry I'm not around to take your calls. Leave a message and I'll get back to you. Maybe.

A beep.

BEN: Hey Fergie. It's Ben. I'm looking for Stace. She's probably with Jenna, so if you see her tell her I need to talk to her. Urgently. Yeah. Thanks, mate.

The phone clicks off.

Blackout or cross-fade into BEN*'s living room. In the room perhaps some Catholic icons are evident. A holy picture. A votive lamp.*

On the radio, 'Good Vibrations' is playing. BEN *walks into the living room in his underpants. He has a large tube of Berocca shoved inside the waistline. He is holding a glass with a Berocca in it. The song fades under.*

VOICE: And you're listening to hits of the sixties and seventies on this Golden Oldie weekend.

BEN goes to turn the radio off, but then he stops and turns it up loud. He listens attentively as he drinks the Berocca. He is caught up in the sentiments of the lyrics.

ZOE enters, unseen, from the kitchen, holding a cup of tea. She watches quietly. BEN *takes a big swig of Berocca, puts his head back, and gargles along with the song. He is putting his heart and soul into it. Just as the music and the gargling reach an emotional high point* BEN *sees* ZOE. *He almost chokes.*

BEN: Jesus Christ.

ZOE: Zoe Brennan.

BEN makes a hasty exit.

Hey, don't get dressed! It was a good look.

BEN reappears in shorts and pulling on a t-shirt. He turns off the radio. He tries to place ZOE.

ZOE: Hi. (*Brief pause.*) This is bizarre, isn't it? We met on Friday night... at the Crystal.

BEN: Oh. Yeah.

ZOE: Cosmic coincidence or what? Anne's your mum right? She was running a bit late for church so she told me to get myself settled in.

BEN: Sorry. You've lost me.

ZOE: I'm your new boarder. The room downstairs? Your fly's undone.

BEN: What?

ZOE laughs at her own joke.

ZOE: I'm renting the room downstairs. I came to see it last week. Anne showed it to me.

BEN: Bullshit.

ZOE: There was a notice on the board at uni. I rang the number and it was Anne. She told me to come around and have a look at the room. So I did. And it's great. Just what I wanted.

BEN: Unfuckingbelievable.

ZOE: Your mum's fantastic. She tells me she works as well as studying part time.

BEN: It's not for rent.

ZOE: Sorry?

BEN: The room. It's not for rent.

ZOE: But Anne said...

BEN: There's been a mistake.

ZOE: No. I've already paid two weeks in advance.

BEN: You'll get your money back. Don't worry about it.

> BEN *guides* ZOE *gently towards the door to the downstairs room.*

BEN: I'll give you a hand with your things.

ZOE: (*pulling away from him*) I don't think so.

BEN: You can't stay here. Sorry.

ZOE: Look, I hate the place I'm in now. I'm sharing with this girl who's bonking a new guy every week. And I always know when they're doing it because she plays Boot Scootin'... at full volume. I love it here. The rent's incredibly reasonable. It's close to uni so it's going to save me heaps on bus fares. Besides which, it's Sunday, it's hard to get a bus, and I've just paid ten bucks to get here by taxi and...

> ANNE *enters. She is carrying her bag and her missal.*

ANNE: Hello.

ZOE: Hi.

ANNE: So, you two have already met.

ZOE: How was church? Have a good pray?

ANNE: Yes thanks.

BEN: What's going on, Mum?

ANNE: How are we going? All settled in?

ZOE: Getting there.

BEN: Mum?

ANNE: Zoe's renting the room downstairs.

BEN: So she tells me.

ANNE: She came to see it last week, didn't you, Zoe. She really likes it.

BEN: When were you planning on letting me in on all this?

ZOE: Look, I might just go and finish with my stuff. I've got a few more things to... you know...

ZOE *begins to exit.* ANNE *calls after her.*

ANNE: Okay, Zo! Just sing out if you need anything.

BEN: You rented the room.

ANNE: She's nice, isn't she?

BEN: Mum?

ANNE: Yes.

BEN: Without talking to me?

ANNE: I was going to.

BEN: After she'd moved in.

ANNE: I knew you'd be angry.

BEN: Yeah, I'm bloody angry actually.

ANNE: Look, it makes sense, renting it out. We could do with the money. She's a godsend really.

BEN: The money.

ANNE: What's wrong?

BEN: It's not like I'm sitting around on my arse all day. I'm trying to get a bloody full-time job. I've applied for three in the last fortnight.

ANNE: I know you have. I wasn't having a go at you.

Pause.

BEN: It's not really the money, is it. Jesus, what are you trying to do, Mum? Find a ring-in for Stacy?

ANNE: That's a terrible thing to say. (*Momentary pause.*) I met Zoe through uni. She seems like a nice girl and she needs somewhere to stay. And we have the room. She's not going to be any trouble.

BEN: God I hope not. You just can't handle trouble.

Brief pause.

ANNE: You better go down and tell her then. Go on. If having her here is going to make you so miserable.

BEN: Please don't start playing the martyr...

ANNE: Tell her to pack up all her things and get out.

BEN: Look. Just forget it, okay? Don't worry about it. It's your house. Rent the room.

The doorbell rings. ANNE *goes to answer it.*

Rent the whole bloody house for all I care. I'll be moving out soon anyway. Shit.

ANNE *returns with* FATHER PAUL, *the parish priest. He is carrying some books. The atmosphere is awkward.* PAUL *would have heard* BEN*'s outburst.*

PAUL: G'day Ben.

BEN: Father.

PAUL *hands the books to* ANNE.

PAUL: I had a scrounge through my books. These are all I came up with.

ANNE: Thank you.

PAUL: I hope they'll be useful. They're donkey's years old some of them, but I think you'll find some interesting stuff in there.

ANNE: They look wonderful. (*To* BEN) I've got a Signs and Meanings presentation coming up at uni. I'm doing it on The Ecstasy of St. Teresa.

BEN *looks at* ANNE.

BEN: (*softly*) Jesus.

ANNE: Paul said he had these books. (*Brief pause.*) Well. I'll just go and put on the jug.

ANNE *puts down the books and exits. There's a moment of silence.*

PAUL: So. How've you been, Ben?

BEN: Oh you know, still totin' that ol' cross.

Brief pause.

PAUL: So what's been happening? Any news on uni?

BEN: What do you mean?

PAUL: Given any thought to going back?

BEN: Nope.

PAUL: That's a pity.

BEN: Not really. I'm doing some work for a mate of mine down the club.

PAUL: Oh yes, that's right, Anne told me. The DJ.

BEN: Fergus, yeah. He's been great.

PAUL: Good. That's good.

ANNE enters.

ANNE: Tea won't be long. Let's all go out on the verandah. It'll be cooler out there.

BEN: I don't want anything.

ANNE: Oh. (*To* PAUL) Well, looks like just you and me then.

ANNE and PAUL exit onto the verandah. BEN *goes to the books on Teresa of Avila. He picks up one of the books and begins to leaf through it.* ZOE *enters. She is holding a large stuffed toy Smurf.*

ZOE: What's the story? Am I in or out?

A pause.

BEN: Where did you find him?

ZOE: In one of the cupboards downstairs.

BEN *holds his hand for the Smurf.* ZOE *teasingly puts it behind her back.*

ZOE: Is he yours?

BEN: Give him to me.

ZOE: He *is* yours.

BEN: He's my sister's. Give him to me.

ZOE: Is that your sister's room?

BEN: Yeah.

ZOE: Where is she?

BEN: Gone to ground.

From the dark, STACY'*s voice is heard.*

STACY: Benny, let me in.

ZOE: What, did she shoot through?

BEN: Yeah.

STACY: Benny, let me in I said.

ZOE *throws the Smurf to* BEN.

ZOE: Listen, I'm sorry about all this. I'll just pack up my things and bugger off.

ZOE *begins to exit.*

BEN: No. Stay.

ZOE: But...

BEN: Mum wants you to stay, so stay.

ZOE: What about you?

BEN: I don't give a fart one way or the other.

ZOE: Well, just until I find somewhere else, okay?

BEN: Suit yourself.

ZOE: Is it alright if I call Cairns? Let the folks know where I am?

BEN: Whatever.

ZOE: Where's the phone?

BEN: In the hall.

ZOE *exits.*

Don't forget to pay for it.

BEN *looks at the Smurf, then leans back and closes his eyes.*

SCENE THREE

Change of lighting state. Cross-fade to BEN's *bedroom.* STACY *enters. It is her fourteenth birthday. She is bubbling with excitement.*

STACY: Oh, don't go back to sleep! Get up!

BEN *yawns.*

BEN: (*yawning*) Ping off.

STACY: Where's my present?

BEN *looks at his watch.*

BEN: (*looking at his watch*) Geez, Stacy. It's six o'clock in the morning.

STACY:

Get up! It's my special day.

BEN *rolls onto his stomach.* STACY *sits on* BEN.

BEN: Ping off!

STACY *bounces up and down energetically as she punches* BEN.

STACY: Fourteen birthday punches... one, two, three, four, five, six...

BEN: Stacy!

BEN *pushes* STACY *off.*

STACY: Where is it?

BEN *has hidden the Smurf inside his shirt. He pretends to give birth to it 'Alien'-style.*

Oh wow! Wow! He's brilliant. Thank you. I didn't think you'd get him for me.

STACY *hugs* BEN.

BEN: He's bum ugly if you ask me. He's a boofhead.

STACY: No, he's a classic.

BEN: Check out his nose. It looks like a dick. (*He sees a medal around* STACY*'s neck.*) What's this?

STACY: St Teresa of Avila. Sister Laurentia at school gave it to me for my birthday.

BEN: (*sarcastic*) Cool prezzie.

STACY: Sister said St Teresa is one of the great women of the church, but at my age she was just a gadabout.

BEN: A what?

STACY: She was vain as. She was always stressing about her hair and nails and stuff. But then she became a nun, and that's when God started talking to her...

BEN: Jesus.

STACY:... and she started having holy ecstasies.

BEN: Holy shit.

STACY: Sister said that when it hit her, it was like this huge eagle was lifting her up on its wings... and she'd elevate up into the air.

BEN: It's 'levitate', dumbo.

STACY: The other nuns used to sit on her to try to keep her down. But the ecstasy was too strong and she'd go rising up. (*She demonstrates with her Smurf.*) One to beam up! Beep, beep, beep!

BEN: Red alert! Saint materializing off the starboard bow!

STACY: Life, but not as we know it, Jim!

BEN: Woop, woop, woop! Arm phasers! Raise shields! Fire photon torpedoes! Pow, pow, pow! She's dead.

STACY: Hey, guess what else?

BEN: Piss off. I want to go back to sleep.

STACY: When she died, nine months later they dug her up, and she hadn't decayed. She'd just turned into the colour of dates.

BEN: Gross.

STACY: And if someone stuck their hand between her shoulder blades, she could still stand up. Like this...

BEN: That's sick.

STACY: But then faithful started chopping bits off her to keep as souvenirs. They took a hand and a foot and pieces of flesh and stuff. To keep as holy morsels.

BEN: Relics.

STACY: Hey, you know that relic Mum's got in her rosary beads? That's a bit of a saint.

BEN: Bullshit. I reckon it's a bit of chook.

STACY: It wouldn't be chook.

BEN: It looks like a bit of gristle.

STACY: Why couldn't it be a bit of a saint?

BEN: Think about it, dummy. It's supply and demand, isn't it? Lots of people want relics, but there's not enough saints to go around. (*Ordering meat from a butcher*) Yeah, mate, I'll have a kilo and a half of saint thanks. Trim the fat! They'd have to be making new saints all the time or they'd run out of stock. It'd be like... hey you! Mind if we make you a saint? Excellent!

　　　BEN pretends to saw off STACY's *hand.*

STACY: Ow!

BEN: Now go away. I'm going back to sleep.

STACY: You can't. We've got to go to seven o'clock Mass.

BEN: I'm not going.

STACY: Why?

BEN: Because I'm not.

STACY: Are you sick?

BEN: No.

STACY: You can't just not go.

BEN: Get lost.

STACY: Why aren't you going?

BEN: I don't believe all that crap any more.

STACY: (*horrified*) What will you say to Mum?

BEN: I'll just tell her.

STACY: She's going to kill you, Ben. She'll absolutely go bonkers.

BEN: Who cares?

STACY: You're going to make trouble on my birthday.

BEN: Tough.

> STACY *belts* BEN *with her* SMURF. BEN *fights back.*

STACY: My brother's a big shit.

BEN: Hey. Cut it out!

STACY: Big shitty brother.

BEN: Stacy, drop dead.

STACY: Why did you have to pick today?

> ANNE *enters.*

ANNE: Is the birthday girl in here?

STACY: Ooow!!

ANNE: Hey, careful, Ben. You'll hurt her.

> STACY *runs to her mother and hugs her.*

Ben. You're not dressed. Are you sick?

BEN: Nuh.

ANNE: Come on then, love. Up you get.

> BEN *stares moodily at* ANNE.

STACY: Ben. It's my birthday. And it's late. You know how Mum hates walking in late.

> BEN *begins to get out of bed.* ANNE *exits. Just before* STACY *exits she turns around with the Smurf and makes it fart politely at* BEN.

SCENE FOUR

Lighting change. The present. BEN *is sitting holding the Smurf.* FATHER PAUL *enters from the verandah.*

PAUL: Your mum's really into this uni thing, isn't she?

BEN: Must be. She's always got her head stuck in her books.

PAUL: She's packing death about giving this presentation.

BEN: Is she? I wouldn't know.

PAUL: Yes, well it is her first one. (*Momentary pause.*) I hear you've got a boarder in the house.

BEN: Funny that. I just heard the same thing.

PAUL: What's she like?

BEN: God knows. I just live here.

PAUL: Anne says she's a nice kid.

BEN: Mum sent you in to arbitrate, did she, Father?

PAUL: I said I'd have a chat to you about it.

BEN: It doesn't concern you. Sorry.

> PAUL *goes to leave.*

This girl. Mum hadn't even told her.

PAUL: About what? (*Brief pause.*) Oh. Right.

BEN: She's moved into her room.

PAUL: Anne just can't bear to see that room empty anymore, Ben. She said it's become an unhappy house and...

BEN: So she actually talks to you about it, does she?

PAUL: Not often.

BEN: She never talks to me about it. Not ever.

PAUL: Do you talk to her?

BEN: I can't talk to her. How can I talk to her? She's screwed up so bloody tight I can't get through to her.

> *Momentary pause.*

PAUL: Why don't you just give this thing a burl and see how it works out? It mightn't be too bad.

BEN: I've already told her to stay, so you can tell Mum she's won.

PAUL: I don't think it's a matter of winning.

BEN: Isn't it?

> ZOE *enters. She hands some money to* BEN.

ZOE: Money for the phone call. Stick it somewhere safe.

PAUL: Hello.

ZOE: Hi.

PAUL: You must be the new boarder.

ZOE: Yeah.

> ZOE *looks at* BEN *for an introduction.*

BEN: This is Father Paul.

ZOE: Zoe. Nice to meet you.

PAUL: You too.

ZOE: So how's business?

PAUL: Oh, fine. And what about you? Looks like you've made yourself at home.

BEN: (*quietly*) Looks that way.

Brief pause.

PAUL: Okay. Well. I suppose I'd better get going. Nice meeting you, Zoe.

ZOE: Yeah, same.

PAUL: Goodbye Ben. Maybe I'll see you at mass one of these days.

BEN: You reckon? Do you remember the last time I was at mass?

PAUL: Yes, I do.

Brief pause.

BEN: I've given up on all that.

PAUL: I'm sorry to hear it.

BEN: Don't be.

Brief pause.

PAUL: Say goodbye to your mum for me.

PAUL *begins to leave.*

BEN: You should come and check out a rave sometime.

PAUL: What was that?

ZOE: He reckons you should come and check out a rave.

PAUL: You think so?

BEN: What I've found there I never found in a church.

PAUL: Is that right?

BEN: Yeah, that's right.

Brief pause.

PAUL: So, what are you finding Ben?

Brief pause.

BEN: You don't explain it. You feel it.

ZOE *erupts in a giggle.* BEN *glares at her.*

PAUL: Oh. Well, maybe we can talk about it sometime.

No response from BEN.

I'll be seeing you.

PAUL *smiles at* ZOE *and exits.*

ZOE: You don't explain it. You feel it.

BEN: Get stuffed.

BEN *goes to exit.*

ZOE: Hey, sorry. Really, I was just taking the piss. Listen, that place where you work, the Crystal?

BEN: What about it?

ZOE: Man, if I could have a mix there one night. A bit of a spin of the old vinyl. I would be so stoked.

BEN: And you're telling me this why?

ZOE: Well, I left a tape with that mate of yours. DJ Fergus?

BEN: You and a thousand others.

ZOE: Yeah. That's why I was hoping you could have a word with him.

BEN: What... about you?

ZOE: Well, at least get him to have a listen to my stuff.

BEN: You wish.

ZOE: Why not?

BEN: For all I know your music might be ratshit.

ZOE: It's not! It's bloody good! I'd even play some of it for you if I thought you could be bothered listening.

ZOE *begins to exit. She stops.*

You don't just feel it. You hear it.

ZOE *exits.* BEN *picks up the Smurf and looks at it. Lights down. Telephone call links next scene.*

SCENE FIVE

Voice over: JENNA*'s call to* BEN. *Music effects under.*

BEN: (*quietly*) Hello.

JENNA: Ben? Jenna.

BEN: Jenna. Is Stacy with you?

JENNA: She's a bit upset. Can we meet you at the club?

BEN: I can be there in thirty minutes. Twenty.

JENNA: We'll see you there.

BEN: Is she alright... ? Jenna?

The phone clicks off.

Lights up on ZOE *and* ANNE. ANNE *is rehearsing her Signs and Meanings lecture for* ZOE. *She is holding her notes for her presentation and is speaking to an imaginary audience.*

ANNE: I'm a bit nervous. The last time I had to present anything to a class was when I brought a dead snake to morning talk at St Joseph's, over thirty years ago.

ANNE looks at ZOE *expecting a laugh.* ZOE *looks doubtful.*

ZOE: I'd cut that bit. Go on.

ANNE: I've chosen as my subject the famous Bernini sculpture of St Teresa of Avila. Teresa was a Spanish mystic who wrote her last book when Shakespeare was just getting into his stride. But her words shine as brightly now as they did when they were first written. (ANNE *reads.*) 'I began to think of the soul as if it were a castle made of a single diamond or very clear crystal in which there are many rooms, just as in Heaven there are many mansions. In the centre and midst of them all is the chiefest mansion, where the most secret things pass between God and the soul.' (*Brief pause.*) And this is where I thought I'd bring up the slide.

ZOE: Of what?

ANNE shows ZOE *the picture on the front of her book.*

ANNE: It's called The Ecstasy of St Teresa.

ZOE: Excuse me?

ANNE: She's having an ecstasy.

ZOE: What?

ANNE: She's having an ecstasy with God.

ZOE erupts in a giggle.

ZOE: With God? She's having an ecstasy with God?

ANNE: Yes, that's the reason I chose this sculpture for my presentation. I wanted to draw parallels between spiritual ecstasy and the drug.

ZOE: Oh. That's good. That's a good thing to do.

ANNE *centres herself and continues reading from her notes.*

ANNE: 'Physically, I believe the effects of ecstasy shown in this sculpture have similarities to the drug-induced state. But while spiritual and drug-induced ecstasy are both altered states of consciousness, a religious ecstasy is attained through meditation, contemplation or physical denial... whereas the drug-induced state gives immediate gratification, loading the senses with chemically induced sensations and perceptions.' (*Brief pause.*) What do you think?

ZOE: It's good.

ANNE: No, about ecstasy.

ZOE: I don't know.

ANNE: It's like... now everything has to be instant. Do you know what I mean? Even ecstasy. They think they can just swallow or snort it or shoot up into their veins. (*Brief pause.*) Have you ever tried it?

ZOE: What? Ecstasy?

ANNE: Yes.

ZOE: Nuh, but I see plenty of people who do. Lots of dudes at dance parties are on e.

ANNE: You go to dance parties?

ZOE: Yeah, course I do. I'm a DJ. Didn't I tell you?

ANNE: No.

ZOE: That's where I met Ben. At the Crystal.

ANNE: And you're telling me you don't take drugs.

ZOE: No way. Dad turned me off doing any of that stuff.

ANNE: Good for him.

ZOE: Heck yeah. He's a real pothead my dad. His whole life revolves around that shit. Got to have his bowl of mull on the table every night or he totally loses it. Abuses the fridge if there's no milk, that kind of crap. Who needs it?

> *Brief pause.*

ANNE: I think Ben does.

ZOE: Does he? I wouldn't know.

> *Brief pause.*

ANNE: If it's not for the drugs, why do you go?

ZOE: Are you kidding? For the music, man. The music's fully excellent. That's what it's all about. And you can go there and you feel totally safe. Not like some of the nightclubs around the place. The music's beyond crap, and you've got these rednecks, pissed out of their brains, trying to feel you up. They think they're such heroes, but they wouldn't be able to get a date off a calendar most of them. (*Brief pause.*) Hey, guess what? Ben's organised a gig for me tonight... at the Crystal.

ANNE: Oh. He didn't tell me.

ZOE: Yeah. It's gonna go off, man. That place is gonna go off.

> *A pause.*

Anyway, what are we doing talking about me? You've got this thing to do. Come on. Off you go.

> ANNE *takes up her notes and goes into her presentation, again referring to the imaginary slide. Light focuses in on* ANNE.

ANNE: 'The word ecstasy comes from the Greek, ekstasis, meaning the flight of the soul from the body. The mystery is... what is it in the human psyche that makes us search for this ecstatic state? Whether we call it communing with God, transcending reality, spinning out, getting high, being out of it, being off your face, having time out... or whatever. All these terms suggest uneasiness, a feeling of disillusionment with reality and a desire to escape. So, the question is not really whether these states are equivalent in any way, but why such states are regarded as desirable.'

SCENE SIX

Lighting change. Music or effects under. Voice over: ANNE *is calling the ambulance.*

VOICE: Fire, police or ambulance?

ANNE: Ambulance. Hurry please! It's my daughter...

> *Change of lighting state. Ambulance siren effect in music.*

> BEN *and* ZOE *are about to enter the Crystal. The 'doof' of the music can be heard from inside the club.* ZOE *is anxious and excited about her first DJ gig at the club.* BEN *is carrying her record box.* ZOE *stares in trepidation at the entrance.*

ZOE: I've changed my mind.

BEN: What?

ZOE: I'm not going in.

BEN: Don't be bloody stupid.

ZOE: What if I make a complete dick of myself in front of Fergus?

BEN: Look, he had a listen to your stuff. He really liked it. He wouldn't be letting you play a set if he didn't like what you do.

ZOE: What did he say?

BEN: I already told you.

ZOE: Tell me again.

BEN: He said he thinks you have a real flair for mixing and...

> JENNA *enters and goes into the club.* BEN *sees her.*

ZOE: What's wrong?

BEN: Nothing.

ZOE: Do you know what time I'll be on?

BEN: No.

ZOE: Listen, thanks for organizing this for me. I really appreciate it.

BEN: Don't thank me. Thank him. Come on.

> BEN *grabs* ZOE *by the arm and they enter the club. Cross-fade lights. Music swells into the full-on club sound.* FERGUS *is spinning his set.* ZOE *is immediately fired with enthusiasm.*

ZOE: (*shouting over the music*) Oh, my God! Ohhhhh, my God! I just got a million goosebumps!

BEN: He's good.

ZOE: That is killer music man! He's a total wizard!

BEN: (*yelling*) Go, Fergus!

ZOE: Shit! Far out, man! That is so great!

> *They listen for a moment longer.* ZOE *is becoming more and more enthused.*

I'm just going to sort through my tracks. When you talk to Fergus, ask him when I'm on.

BEN: Okay.

> ZOE *exits to the fire escape.* BEN *begins to dance. After some moments he becomes aware of* JENNA *dancing a little way from him. He tries to ignore her, but without success. Finally he goes to her. They are shouting over the music.*

JENNA: Ben.

BEN: I want to talk to you.

JENNA: What about?

BEN: What about?

JENNA: I can't...

BEN: Get outside.

JENNA: No.

> BEN *grabs hold of* JENNA *and tries to move her.* JENNA *pulls away. She is afraid.*

BEN: Get outside!

JENNA: Screw you, you prick!

> BEN *drags* JENNA *out on the fire escape.* ZOE *is sitting on an upper level of the fire escape going through her vinyl records, choosing which tracks she's going to play in her set. She is unseen by* JENNA *and* BEN. *She witnesses their conversation.*

BEN: Why did you leave her?

JENNA: I don't know.

BEN: Bullshit!

JENNA: Do you think I would have left her if I'd known? She was my friend.

BEN: Shoot it up your arse, Jenna.

JENNA: Fuck you! She was my best friend!

BEN: Sure she was.

JENNA: What makes you so virtuous you think you can judge me?

BEN: (*threatening*) Shut up.

JENNA: People make their own choices. She couldn't handle it. Some can, some can't, and she... Shit! I can't deal with it. I feel like I'm going out of my head.

BEN: (*momentarily sympathetic*) Jesus, Jenna. Why did you just piss off out of it like that?

JENNA: I'm sorry.

BEN: Why did you do that Jenna?

JENNA: I was scared.

BEN: You were what?

JENNA: I was scared. I didn't know what to...

BEN: You were fucking scared? What kind of shit is that?

BEN *goes to grab hold of* JENNA.

JENNA: No!

BEN *stops himself from taking out his anger on* JENNA. *In his rage he begins to smash into the railings of the fire escape. It is as much rage against himself and his own fear as it is against* JENNA. JENNA *is terrified.* ZOE *rushes to her.* FERGUS *appears.*

ZOE: Ben! Ben! Stop it!

FERGUS *grabs* BEN *and tries to calm him.*

FERGUS: Ben! Ben, hey! Come on, man. Stop.

BEN: (*coming back to reality*) Jesus, I'm sorry.

FERGUS: It's okay... it's okay. Just cool it.

FERGUS *helps* BEN *to sit down.*

(*To* JENNA) You alright?

JENNA *nods.*

FERGUS: You sure? (*Gently to* BEN) What were you doing, man?

BEN: I don't know.

Pause.

FERGUS: Listen, this has been bad for you. Nobody's saying it hasn't. But you're not the only one. Try to understand how hard this has been for Jenna too. Jenn and Stace... they were really good mates. (*Momentary pause.*) Oh, come on, man. I just hate to see this happening. You're part of my life but she's part of it too. It's been rough sailing for everyone, but life goes on. You have to try and put all this behind you and just get on with it. Okay?

FERGUS *turns to* JENNA.

Go and wait for me inside Jenn. I won't be long.

JENNA *is about to exit into the club. She stops.*

JENNA: I know how much you loved her, Ben, but I loved her too.

JENNA *exits.*

ZOE: Are you all right, Ben?

FERGUS *has forgotten about* ZOE *being there.*

FERGUS: Hey, thank you. It's good you were around.

ZOE: I was just sorting through my tracks.

FERGUS: (*about her hair*) Love your little...

ZOE: Thanks. (*To* BEN) You sure you're all right?

FERGUS: He's okay. Just let him be.

> *Brief pause.*

ZOE: Have you got idea when I'll be going on?

FERGUS: Sorry?

ZOE: I've got loads of amazing stuff. I'll show you.

> ZOE *dashes up to where she left her records. She brings them down to show to* FERGUS.

I usually play a bit of a mixed bag because people go off harder with a good mix. So I thought I'd start with...

FERGUS: Whoa. Hang on a minute. What are you talking about?

ZOE: What I'll be playing for my set.

FERGUS: (*looking at* BEN) What's going on man?

BEN: I thought you said she could have a mix tonight.

FERGUS: I said if any of the other DJs didn't show maybe she could have a mix tonight. But that hasn't happened. Everyone's turned up.

BEN: Shit.

FERGUS: Hello! That was the deal, remember?

BEN: I'm sorry, Zoe. I must have misunderstood.

ZOE: This is a joke, right?

FERGUS: 'Fraid not.

ZOE: Yeah, that's really funny. Were you setting me up?

FERGUS: I'll organize it for some other time, all right, babe?

ZOE: You guys are all the same. Your bloody testosterone warps your brain and you think you're God's gift to music. You think girls can't play the decks. You think everything we spin is tamer than the stuff you do. Well, that's just a load of macho crap. My stuff's as good as yours any day. Better. By the way, don't call me babe.

FERGUS: Okay.

ZOE: Dickhead.

> ZOE *exits into the club.*

FERGUS: She wants me.

BEN: What a shithouse night this has turned out to be.

FERGUS: You shouldn't have promised her she'd be going on man.

BEN: I screwed up. I'm always screwing up.

> *Pause.*

FERGUS: I'll see if I can arrange for her to play another night. Her music's not bad. It's different. (*Momentary pause.*) Hey, do you remember my first gig in this place?

BEN: Yeah. It was Stacy's first time here too.

FERGUS: That's right. Shit, so it was. Wasn't that a magic night.

> STACY*'s voice from the dark.*

STACY: I want to go in.

> BEN *puts his head in his hands.*

FERGUS: You okay matey? How are you feeling?

STACY: I want to dance.

BEN: You got any gear?

FERGUS: That's entirely possible. Come with Fergus.

> BEN *and* FERGUS *exit into the club. Change of lighting state and music to denote passing of time. Light up on* BEN *lost in his own world.* STACY *moves into* BEN*'s light.*

SCENE SEVEN

BEN *moves* STACY *gently out of the light. They are outside the club, standing conspiratorially close together.* STACY *has the Smurf in her backpack. The distant 'doof' of music from the club resonates into the street.* STACY *is bursting with excitement.* BEN *looks around and then speaks quietly to her. It is like a catechism.*

STACY: You're a legend, Ben. This is so cool.

BEN: Just settle down, okay? And listen. So what do you have to do?

STACY: Drink plenty of water.

BEN: And... ?

STACY: Don't guzzle it. Just sip it.

BEN: Because?

STACY: Too much is just as bad as too little.

BEN: Have you got some money? No.

BEN *hands over some money to* STACY.

You'll have to buy it. There's no cold water in the toilets.

STACY: Why not?

BEN: They turn it off.

STACY: Why?

BEN: Why do you think, dummy? So you have to pay rip-off prices at the bar.

STACY: How rude.

BEN: So buy some water and make sure you drink it. You can dehydrate.

STACY: All right.

BEN: And don't let yourself get overheated. Make sure you chill out every now and again, okay?

STACY: Hey, I'll be chilling out, man.

BEN: Stacy, listen. The e could make you a bit sick at first. You might want to spew.

STACY: (*making the Smurf graphically throw up*) Blahhhhhh!

BEN: Stacy. Are you listening to me?

STACY: Yes.

BEN: There's something else I told you. What was it?

STACY *looks blank.*

Only ever get e's from people you trust.

STACY: Right.

BEN: Because?

STACY: You don't know what some of that other stuff is cut with. Hey, stop worrying, Ben... you'll look after me. Mum's always saying...

BEN: Jesus, don't you tell mum about this.

STACY: As if.

BEN: I took you to the pictures.

STACY: Yeah. Come on, I want to go in. I want to dance.

BEN *looks around. He breaks the e in half as if breaking the host at communion.*

STACY: Only half?

BEN: It's your first time.

STACY: (*whining*) Ohhhh.

The following is secretive. The ritualistic sharing of the sacrament. BEN *secretly puts the half tablet in his own mouth. He then puts the other half in* STACY*'s mouth. She holds the tablet there for a moment. It tastes horrible. She shudders and makes a face.*

STACY: Oh, yuk!

BEN *hands her his water bottle and she quickly takes a drink.*

STACY: All gone! When does it start working?

BEN: Soon.

STACY: Come on. I want to go in.

BEN: Okay. Now don't eye contact the bouncers. Just stick with me, act cool and do exactly what I say.

They move towards the entrance to the club.

Lighting change and music swells up. STACY *sees* JENNA *and runs to her. They throw their arms around each other in delight.* FERGUS *takes the stand to play his first set at the Crystal.*

VOICE-OVER: And now, making his very first appearance at the Crystal... the totally wicked DJ Fergus!

JENNA, STACY *and* BEN *cheer and scream for* FERGUS *as he begins to spin. They dance.*

Light down to focus on BEN. STACY *moves into his light. She latches onto* BEN *and holds him tight.*

STACY: Hug me!

BEN: Look out! Klingon ship decloaking off the starboard bow.

STACY: I've got wings Benny! I'm flying!

STACY *joins her hands and raises her eyes heavenward.*

Hey. Guess who?

BEN: (*space control*)... and the Eagle has landed. And he's picking her up. Four, three, two, one. And yes... we have lift-off.

STACY: Beep, beep, beep. One to beam up.

BEN: And she's levitating. She's levitating. We have the technology.

STACY: Engage the warp drive.

BEN: And she's going ballistic. Yeah, she's goin' off.

BEN *lifts* STACY *up.*

...and she's sailin' among the stars, man.

STACY: She's headin' straight for heaven.

> *As* STACY *flies upward for a moment she mirrors the rapturous image of the Bernini sculpture. Text over music. 'Take me up on Eagle's Wings' repeating over and over.* STACY *moves out of* BEN*'s light and disappears.*

SCENE EIGHT

> BEN *is left alone, coming out of a trance-like state. The music changes to something with a comic feel. Gradually* BEN *becomes aware of* ZOE *dancing nearby.* BEN *begins to intrude playfully on* ZOE*'s space, blowing his whistle, teasing her.* ZOE *tries to ignore him without success. Finally she leaves the dance floor and moves out onto the fire escape.* BEN *follows her.*

ZOE: Go away. You suck, officially.

> BEN *screeches like a wounded monkey.*

Yes, folks, living proof that evolution can go in reverse.

> BEN *sidles up to* ZOE *and takes her hand.*

Go to hell.

BEN: (*Lucifer voice*) Oh, but I'm already there. Come with us, Zoe. Come with us.

ZOE: Bugger off.

BEN: Aren't we ever going to talk again?

ZOE: Probably, just not to each other.

> *Music from inside the club changes. There has been a switch-over of DJs.*

BEN: Sorry about before. I feel really bad about it.

ZOE: Get over it.

BEN: I must have got my wires crossed.

> *Brief pause.*

ZOE: What's the story with that girl... that Jenna?

BEN: Do you mind if we don't? I'm not in the mood.

Brief pause.

ZOE: Where's Stacy, Ben?

BEN: Listen, about the gig...

ZOE: I said forget it.

BEN: Fergus says he'll give you a go another night.

ZOE: Excuse me? Give me a go? I'm an experienced DJ!

BEN: Yeah, sorry. Hey did I tell you he's been invited to guest at the Revelation party in Sydney next month? It's going to be massive.

ZOE: I'm thrilled.

BEN: Yeah, he's really building up a bit of a rep for himself. He wants to try and crack it overseas. Become an international DJ. He reckons he'd go down well in the States.

ZOE: And when's he scheduled for his humility transplant?

FERGUS *enters with tickets for the rave. He doesn't expect to see* ZOE.

ZOE: Well, speak of the devil.

BEN: Hey, Fergie.

FERGUS: It's okay, I'll catch you later.

BEN *sees the tickets in* FERGUS' *hand.*

BEN: Whatcha got there?

FERGUS *hands the tickets to* BEN.

FERGUS: Freebies for the rave. You did a great job with the flyers. We've got heaps of interest. Thanks, matey.

ZOE: What rave?

BEN: Happenin' tomorrow night. Fergie's organised it.

BEN *has a flier in his pocket. He hands it to* ZOE.

ZOE: (*reading*) 'A Rave New World. Happening somewhere on the coast. Brothers and sisters, elevate your souls to new dimensions and synchronize your bodies with the rhythms of the universe. Featuring the extraordinary mixing wizardry of one of the country's most respected sound masters, the legendary DJ Ferg-arse.' So who wrote this?

FERGUS: I did.

ZOE: Man, your reality check has bounced.

FERGUS: Think you could write better?

ZOE: If I swallowed a pen, my arse could write better.

FERGUS: Then you'd be a smart arse.

> BEN *and* FERGUS *laugh.*

ZOE: So where's it going to be?

> FERGUS *smiles enigmatically.*

Oooh, so it's a big secret.

FERGUS: Number's on the flyer. I expect you'll be gracing us with your presence?

ZOE: Nuh. Can't afford it.

FERGUS: Pity, it's going to be awesome. Hey, listen. I'm sorry about the mix-up before. Did Ben tell you I'm arranging for you to play a set another night?

ZOE: Yeah, sure.

FERGUS: No, I mean it. I really like your music. It's... distinctive. So, come on. Why don't we just kiss and make up?

ZOE: I'd rather kiss dog shit.

FERGUS: Whatever makes you tingle.

> FERGUS *and* BEN *laugh.* ZOE *makes a rude sign at* FERGUS *and exits.*

FERGUS: (*as Prospero*) Oh, rave new world that has such creatures in it!

> STACY *moves into the light.* FERGUS *checks his watch.*

Hey, I'm on again.

STACY: This is the best night since I've been alive.

> FERGUS *begins to exit.*

FERGUS: Comin' in?

STACY: I don't ever want it to end.

FERGUS: Ben?

BEN: What?

FERGUS: I'm on again. My next set.

BEN: Oh, yeah. I'll be there in a minute.

> FERGUS *exits.* BEN *is alone with* STACY.

STACY: Promise you'll bring me here again.

BEN: I'm not promising anything.

STACY: But you might.

BEN: I might.

STACY: Yes!

> STACY *looks up at the stars.*

Wow. The stars are so amazing.

BEN: (*looking up*) You should see them when there's no other lights around. Like this time I was way out in the bush? You should have seen 'em then.

STACY: Yeah?

> *Brief pause.*

BEN: You know how normally the stars look like this kind of... crystal sphere around the earth? Well, on this night, it was like there was infinite depth. And they seemed to just go on and on. And when you kept looking, you could almost see star trails connecting them together. It was like... if you could join up the dots you'd see the constellations.

STACY: Wow.

> *Brief pause.*

What's that one called?

BEN: Which?

STACY: That one. The really, really bright one.

BEN: That's Sirius.

STACY: It's brilliant.

BEN: Yeah. Sirius is the brightest star in the sky.

STACY: So, that's you, then.

BEN: What?

> *Brief pause.*

STACY: And what's that one?

BEN: Where?

STACY: That little one. See? That dull little one.

BEN: The little ones don't have names. They just have numbers.

STACY: Oh.

> *A pause.*

BEN: Anyway, that star isn't really little and dull. It just looks like that because it's so far away. If you got up very close to it, it'd be gigantic. And probably a thousand times brighter than Sirius.

STACY: Really?

BEN: Hell yeah. A thousand times brighter.

Brief pause.

STACY: Hug me.

BEN *puts his arm around* STACY. *They continue looking at the stars.*

SCENE NINE

Voice over: FERGUS *is at a gig. He answers* BEN*'s call on his mobile phone. He is trying to hear* BEN*'s voice over the music.*

FERGUS: Fergus.

BEN: Fergie, where are you, man?

FERGUS: At the gig. I'm just about to go on again.

BEN: Stacy's in hospital.

FERGUS: What?

BEN: Stacy's in hospital. She's done too much shit. She's really sick.

FERGUS: Fuck.

BEN: They need to know what she's taken. She was with Jenna. I need to talk to Jenna. Have you seen her?

FERGUS: No. No I haven't.

BEN: Shit.

FERGUS: Listen, if I do see her, I'll tell her to get in touch with you. Where are you?

BEN: The Mater. Emergency. Tell her to hurry.

FERGUS: All right mate. You hang in there, okay?

BEN: Yeah.

Phone clicks off. Lighting change. The church. Techno-type 'ambulance siren' music blends into the last moments of the hymn 'On Eagle's Wings' sung by the cantor as the congregation leave the church. ANNE *sits alone in the church.* FATHER PAUL *approaches her. He is holding the pyx with the communion host.*

PAUL: Hello. This is a bit unusual for you, isn't it, Saturday Mass?

ANNE: I'll be studying all day tomorrow. I've got that presentation.

PAUL: Oh yes, I'd forgotten. I'll be thinking of you.

ANNE: I'd rather you prayed for me. I'll need all the help I can get.

PAUL: I need some help too actually, with communion to the sick. I know you're not rostered on for this month, but Mrs. Taylor's not well again and...

ANNE: That's okay. I'll do it.

> PAUL *hands* ANNE *the pyx.*

PAUL: Thanks.

> ANNE *presses her hand against her eyes.*

PAUL: Are you all right?

ANNE: I've got a headache.

PAUL: I'm not surprised. You're snowed under at work, and now you've taken on all this study.

ANNE: I like to keep busy.

> *Brief pause.*

PAUL: How's the boarder working out?

ANNE: Zoe? She's lovely. She's settling in really well.

PAUL: What about Ben? Are they getting on okay?

ANNE: They seem to be. Ben's arranged for her to play some music tonight down at that club.

PAUL: Oh. Well that's good. (*Brief pause.*) How is Ben?

ANNE: Fine. (*Brief pause.*) No, I don't know really. We don't communicate.

PAUL: Yes, well, I hear the same story from a lot of parents. So I wouldn't be too...

ANNE: You know he blames it all on me.

PAUL: Sorry?

ANNE: What happened with Stacy. He thinks it was all my fault.

PAUL: I'm sure he doesn't.

ANNE: Oh no, he does. He thinks I handled things very badly.

PAUL: You did what you thought was right.

ANNE: Yes.

> *Brief pause.*

PAUL: Stop being so hard on yourself, Anne. I know how you must be feeling but...

ANNE: I'm sorry, Paul, you wouldn't have a clue how I'm feeling. Not unless you've got some kids stashed away somewhere that we don't know about.

PAUL: Anne...

ANNE: I know. You're only trying to help. Everybody was always only trying to help. But no one actually did anything. Not even you.

PAUL: What did you expect me to do, Anne? March into your house and start laying down the law about how she should live her life? I couldn't do that. (*Brief pause.*) People expect me to have all the answers, but I don't. I'm like everyone else. I'm trying to learn by going where I have to go.

Brief pause.

ANNE: I'm sorry.

PAUL: So am I.

ANNE: I'm so sorry.

PAUL: Listen, we're good friends, aren't we? I'd hate to think you couldn't be honest with me.

ANNE: I'd hate that too.

Change of lighting state. STACY *is standing in a pool of light.*

STACY: Mum? I won't do it again. I promise.

PAUL: I'm always here. Whenever you need someone to talk to...

ANNE: I know. Thank you.

STACY: Mum? Say something.

Brief pause.

PAUL: So, on your way home now?

STACY: I love you, Mum.

ANNE: I'll just stay a moment longer, if that's okay.

PAUL: See you soon.

PAUL *puts his hand on* ANNE's *shoulder for a moment. He exits.*

SCENE TEN

STACY *has come home from school after being expelled for smoking pot.* ANNE *is staring at her in silence.* STACY *is deeply upset.*

STACY: I won't do it again. I promise.

>   *Silence.*

Mum?

>   *Silence.*

I'm really, *really* sorry. Mum? Say something.

ANNE: I don't know what to say to you, Stacy. You must think I'm really dumb. Poor old mum. Thick as two short planks. I've been doing drugs and you've had absolutely no idea.

STACY: I smoked some pot, that's all. It's no big deal.

ANNE: Stacy, they will not have you back. You can't go back to school. Do you understand?

STACY: I don't care. Why would I want to go back? What's the point?

ANNE: Stacy...

STACY: Anyway, I'm not the only one who does it. Lots of kids go out for a choof at lunchtime. I was just unlucky.

ANNE: Unlucky.

STACY: I'm sorry.

ANNE: It's a bit late for that. Obviously this is why your schoolwork's been going down the drain.

>   *A pause.*

Have you been taking money out of my purse?

STACY: What?

ANNE: Have you been taking money? To buy drugs?

STACY: No.

ANNE: Yesterday I had twenty dollars in my purse. It wasn't there this morning. Twenty dollars just doesn't walk out of my purse, Stacy.

>   *Brief pause.*

STACY: I borrowed it.

ANNE: You borrowed it.

STACY: I was going to put it back.

ANNE: Oh, Stacy.

STACY: I was.

> *Brief pause.*

ANNE: What other drugs are you taking?

STACY: As if. I'm not stupid.

ANNE: Are you telling me the truth?

STACY: Yes, I swear.

ANNE: I wish I could believe you.

STACY: You don't trust me.

ANNE: I just don't understand all this. It's not like you to...

STACY: (*bursting into tears*) I don't want to be like me!

> *A pause.*

ANNE: Stacy... come on. Come on, love. Don't cry. Please don't cry.

STACY: I'm sorry.

ANNE: Are you?

STACY: Yes. I won't do it again.

ANNE: You have to promise me, Stacy.

STACY: I promise.

ANNE: No, I mean it. You have to promise that's the end of it. I can't have this. I will not have this.

STACY: I promise, Mum. I love you.

ANNE: I love you too.

> *Lighting change.* STACY *has gone.* ANNE *is left alone in the church.*

SCENE ELEVEN

Cross-fade lighting. ANNE *is at home studying.* BEN *enters.*

BEN: Keeping vigil are we, Mum?

ANNE: I went to evening Mass. I decided I'd stay up and do some study. (*Brief pause.*) How was the club?

BEN: I wish you wouldn't do this.

ANNE: What?

BEN: Waiting up until five in the morning, for God's sake.

ANNE: Ben, I have been studying.

BEN: Checking up on me all the time. As if you really give a shit.

ANNE: I've got a presentation to give at uni. It's my first one and I want to do well. That is why I am sitting up. So please don't come home and start hammering at me. I've got a headache.

ANNE turns her attention to her books.

BEN: That's right. Hide away in your bloody books.

ANNE: Ben! For Heaven's sake! Go to bed and sleep off... whatever it is you've taken. Just look at you.

BEN: Look at me? Shit, Mum. Look at you.

ANNE again pretends to go back to her study. She leafs through one of her books. BEN watches her for some moments.

What are you looking for?

ANNE: Something. I thought I'd found something, but I've lost it.

She closes her book. She stands and begins to gather up her study materials.

What's up with Zoe? She seemed very down when she came in.

BEN: She didn't get to play her set.

ANNE: Why?

BEN: I don't know. Something screwed up.

ANNE: I thought you'd promised her she'd be doing it. She was really looking forward to it.

BEN: Yeah, I know.

ANNE: She said you'd organised it. She'd bought this thing for her hair.

BEN: Yeah, I know, Mum. I screwed up. Okay?

ANNE: Why doesn't that surprise me, Ben?

BEN: What's that supposed to mean?

A pause.

ANNE: Why do you keep doing it? How can you after... ?

BEN: Do what? What are you talking about?

ANNE: You know very well what I'm talking about. Does it really make you so happy?

BEN: No. But at least it's time out. It least it gives me some fucking time out. From you.

Both BEN and ANNE are deeply wounded by BEN's words. ANNE exits.

Mum? Mum? Yeah go on. Just shut me out. Slam the door on me too! That always works when you don't know what else to do, doesn't it, Mum.

> BEN *puts a CD on the player. 'Magic Carpet'. He puts his earphones on and turns the music up loud. He sits down and closes his eyes.*

SCENE TWELVE

Music up into next scene. Change of lighting state. STACY*'s room.* STACY *is there with* JENNA. *They are playing 'Magic Carpet' on a portable CD player and smoking pot (a bong). There are a number of empty stubbies scattered around. A large stuffed Smurf is also present.* STACY*'s body language reveals that she's smoking to try to come down from too much speed. There's urgency in the way she's smoking. She's on edge, irritable.* BEN *enters.*

BEN: Hey! Turn that bloody music down!

STACY: Benny!

BEN: Turn it down! I'm trying to watch TV up there.

STACY: (*turning the music down*) Jenn and I are having a session. Wanna join us?

BEN: How dumb are you? You can smell it all over the house. If Mum comes home, you're rooted.

STACY: Mummy's working late, dummy.

JENN: Hey, Ben. What do you get when you drink wet cement? Stoned. Get it?

BEN: Get real, Jenna.

JENN: Hey, this is my reality, man.

STACY: Want some goeey, Benny? We've got some.

JENN: Yeah, come on. Go, go, goeey.

BEN: Shut up, Jenna. You're an idiot. You're off your face.

STACY: We're off our tits!

BEN: Stacy...

STACY: Benedict...

JENN: Benedict! Whoa!

BEN: You're doing way too much of that stuff. You should watch it.

STACY: (*making a rude gesture*) You should watch this.

BEN: You'll shoot your brain.

STACY: Pow! Pow! Duh.

JENN: I think you should mind your own business.

BEN: Everything you think is bullshit, Jenna. You open your mouth and a pile of crap pours out.

STACY: I need this. It's bringing me down. Okay? I need it.

BEN: Yeah, because of the speed, dumb bum. That stuff sucks.

JENNA: And he never touches anything I suppose.

STACY: Crap.

BEN: At least I'm in control. At least I don't...

STACY: Blah blah blah blah blah...

BEN: (*looks at his watch*) It's five fifteen. Remember what Mum said last time? If you're sprung again, she'll...

STACY: I told you. She's working late. It's Thursday.

BEN: It's Friday, Stacy.

STACY: You're beginning to seriously piss me off, Ben. Have a hit of this and shut up.

> ANNE*'s voice is heard. She has arrived home from work and is coming downstairs.*

ANNE: Stacy? Stacy!

BEN: Oh, shit.

ANNE: What's going on down there?

> *There's an unsuccessful scramble to hide the bong and get rid of the smoke.* ANNE *enters.* STACY *is looking angelic.*

STACY: Hello, Mummy.

JENN: Love the shirt.

> *Pause.*

ANNE: What are you doing?

STACY: Well... I'm probably sitting here in my room listening to CDs with Jenna.

ANNE: You're smoking that stuff again.

STACY: Why did you ask if you already knew?

ANNE: Don't speak to me like that.

STACY: Jesus Christ.

ANNE: And don't blaspheme.

STACY: Settle down, Mum. Just chill out a bit.

ANNE: I will not 'chill out' a bit! I am sick to death of it, Stacy.

> ANNE *sees the bong.*

What's this? Is this one of those... pongs?

> JENNA, STACY *and* BEN *look at each other.*

JENN: Hey. Somebody light my pong.

> JENN *makes a disgusting fart noise and pretends to light it. She dramatically self destructs.* STACY *and* BEN *convulse. They are in agony.*

ANNE: Stop it!

> *Sudden silence.*

BEN: Sorry, Mum.

ANNE: Stacy, you're seventeen. What do you think you're doing to yourself, smoking this stuff?

STACY: It's just pot, Mum. Everybody does it.

JENN: Yeah. Everybody pongs. Phew.

> JENNA *laughs.*

BEN: Shut up moron.

ANNE: I don't care what everybody does. I will not have drugs in this house.

STACY: Had a look in your bathroom cupboard lately? It's a bloody chemist shop.

BEN: Knock it off, Stacy.

ANNE: You lied to me. Stacy! Look at me when I'm speaking to you.

> STACY *looks at her.*

You lied to me. You told me you weren't going to do this any more, and I put my faith in you.

STACY: I'm sorry. Okay?

ANNE: I've said it to you I don't know how many times before. And it's the last time I'll say it. This is my house, and while you're living here you will abide by my rules. I will not have you using drugs. I've got another child to consider.

BEN: (*quietly*) Shit, Mum.

JENNA *looks at* BEN *and sniggers.*

ANNE: Where are you getting the money to buy all this stuff anyway?

ANNE *looks at* JENNA.

Are you giving it to her?

JENN: I'll see ya, Stace.

JENNA *exits.*

ANNE: I don't ever again want to see her anywhere near this place. I've never liked you being friends with that girl.

STACY: You can't stop me from seeing my friends.

ANNE: She's a no-hoper.

STACY: How would you know? You don't know her. You've never taken the time to get to know her.

ANNE: I don't even know *you* anymore. I don't know who you are.

STACY: I'm a loser junkie dope fiend. That's who you think I am.

ANNE: That's not true.

STACY: It is. It is.

ANNE: Stacy listen to me. You've been blessed with a wonderful life...

STACY: Oh, here we go...

ANNE:... and you're wasting it. You're throwing it away.

STACY: Bor-ring!

ANNE: Why don't you go out find something worthwhile to do? I don't know. At least try to find yourself some kind of job instead of just sitting around here all day...

STACY'*s speed induced hysteria takes over.*

STACY: Oh, fuck off, for Christ's sake!

BEN: Stacy.

ANNE: What did you say to me?

STACY: You heard.

ANNE: Don't you ever speak to me like that again or I'll...

STACY: Or you'll what? Crucify me? Fuck off! Come on then, Mum.

STACY *spreads her arms.*

Bang, bang, bang, bang!

BEN: Stacy. Stop it.

ANNE *is horrified. She moves towards* STACY.

STACY: No! You just fucking stay away from me. Don't you fucking come near me. Don't fucking talk to me. I don't need this now. I don't want to listen to any more of your fucking crap!

ANNE: I don't know what's happening here. (*To* BEN) Can somebody tell me what's happening?

BEN: It'll be okay, Mum. Just let me talk to her.

STACY: Shit! No wonder dad hit the piss. No wonder he fucked off. Nag, nag, fucking nag, nag, nag. I don't know how he put up with it for so long. Put up with you!

BEN: Stacy!

ANNE: Get out.

BEN: No, Mum.

ANNE: I want you out of here. Now.

STACY: I'm going.

BEN: Look this is stupid. Can everyone just... stop this? Please.

> STACY *drags out a bag and starts to hurl things randomly into it.* BEN *tries to stop her.*

BEN: Mum? Can we just stop this?

ANNE: I don't want you back in this house. Not until you stop using those dirty filthy drugs.

> STACY *picks up the Smurf and hurls it at* BEN.

STACY: Hey, Ben. You can have old Boofhead. I'm bequeathing him to you.

ANNE: Do you hear me, Stacy?

STACY: Give the rest of my stuff to St Vinnies. Or burn it.

> STACY *staggers to the door, things hanging out of a hastily-packed bag.*

ANNE: And I don't want you back until you can treat me with some respect.

STACY: That'll be never.

> STACY *exits.* BEN *goes to follow her.* ANNE *stops him.*

ANNE: No! Don't you dare go after her! Don't you dare! I've had it! She'll come back after she's dried out, or whatever it is they do, for a couple of days. She'll come running back. Just leave her.

> BEN *and* ANNE *are left alone.*

SCENE THIRTEEN

Change of lighting state. Fade up music 'Magic Carpet'. BEN *is still sitting listening to the CD with his earphones on, but the music is blaring.*

ZOE *is returning from having a shower. She is in her dressing-gown. She picks up the end of* BEN*'s earphones and shows it to him.*

ZOE: (*yelling*) It works better if you plug it in!

    ZOE *goes to turn the music down.*

BEN: Leave it.

ZOE: It's too loud.

BEN: I like it loud.

ZOE: Well, I don't... (*turning down the volume*)... and I'm paying rent here so it's just as much my house as yours. Anyway, Anne's been up all night studying. She's probably trying to get some sleep.

BEN: Who gives a shit?

ZOE: What's wrong with you, you sook?

BEN: Sook?

ZOE: Yeah, what's your problem?

BEN: She's pissing me right off.

ZOE: Geez, what is it with you two, Ben?

BEN: I don't think that's any of your business, Zoe.

ZOE: Oh, he's in another one of his pissy moods. How unusual.

BEN: Shut up.

ZOE: Take a risk Ben. Talk to me.

BEN: Jesus Christ.

ZOE: You obviously need to talk to someone. I mean, you and Anne never seem to communicate with each other. And you should. I really think it'd help you both to...

BEN: Who the hell do you think you are, Zoe? You've been in this fucking house two minutes and you think you can psychoanalyse everybody. Offer everybody all this bloody advice. How would you know what would or wouldn't help us? Why don't you just piss off out of it and leave us alone.

ZOE: Oh go... suck your gums! You... freakazoid!

ZOE and BEN stare at each other in silence for a moment. Then BEN begins to laugh.

Don't you dare laugh at me.

BEN tries to touch ZOE.

BEN: Zoe...

ZOE: (*pulling away*) No. Leave me alone! I'm having an emotional outburst.

BEN: I'm an arsehole.

ZOE: Mega.

BEN: I'm sorry.

ZOE: Sometimes you're okay and other times you're a real hound dog. What's real with you?

ZOE goes to exit. BEN calls after her.

BEN: Hey, listen. What about this Rave New World thing that Fergus is organising?

ZOE: (*stopping*) What about it?

BEN: Are we going?

ZOE: You might be. I've got no money.

BEN takes out his tickets and waves them tantalisingly.

BEN: It's got your name on it.

ZOE: Don't do me any favours.

BEN: I'm not. I'd really like you to come.

ZOE: Well, I can't. I've got to vacuum my room...

BEN: Hey that's always fun.

ZOE:... and I've got a lot of study to do.

BEN: Pity. It's going to be excellent.

ZOE: Is it?

BEN: With old Fergie running the show? You bet. I remember he organised this full moon forest party once...

ZOE: I've played at those foresty things. Up in Cairns.

BEN: Yeah? Anyway, to get to this one you had to walk down this kind of pathway through the bush. There were hundreds and hundreds of people, all walking through the trees together at night. So, we get to the place, and we're setting up the sound system. And then this huge bloody moon comes out from behind a cloud and starts shining up the sky. And there are these gigantic trees all around us. Then old Fergie starts spinning his tracks, and suddenly, these great swarms of fruit bats just rise up out of the trees. I don't know who got the biggest shock, us or them. That was a miraculous night, man. These great black clouds of fruit bats... just hooning on past the moon.

Music begins to swell up to link into next scene.

BEN: So will you come?

SCENE FOURTEEN

The sacristy of the church. Sounds of organ notes fade away. FATHER PAUL *is taking off his stole and folding it.* ANNE *enters the sacristy.*

ANNE: Father...

PAUL: Hello. I didn't expect to see you this morning. Aren't you supposed to be studying?

ANNE: I can't do this.

PAUL: What?

ANNE: I can't take communion to the sick.

> ANNE *hands the pyx to* FATHER PAUL.

I'm sorry.

> ANNE *begins to exit.* PAUL *stops her gently.*

PAUL: Anne, wait a moment.

ANNE: I've got to get home. I've got this presentation.

PAUL: Tell me what's wrong.

ANNE: I just can't do this anymore. I can't.

> *Brief pause.*

PAUL: Anne, she's in God's hands...

ANNE: No. She's dead. That's it. She's gone. There are times when it just catches me by surprise, you know? It's like someone has their fist pressing here. Pressing really hard. Pressing so hard I can barely breathe.

PAUL: Why don't we just pray gently and... ?

ANNE: Pray to who? All He's ever done is take everything I ever cared about away from me.

PAUL: Anne, listen...

ANNE: Why? There's nothing you can say that will help. Not unless you can make me understand why she went and why I'm losing my son. (*Brief pause.*) You can't.

>ANNE *exits.*

SCENE FIFTEEN

Change of lighting state. Music up. The Rave New World event. BEN *and* ZOE *are on the beach. Storm clouds are scudding across the moon. In the distance, the sounds of the rave.*

VOICE-OVER

MUSIC: Sometimes a thousand twangling instruments
                       Will hum about mine ears; and sometimes voices...

>*Sounds of sampled singing voices swell up over the music.*

                       That, if I then had waked after long sleep,
                       Will make me sleep again: and then, in dreaming,
                       The clouds methought would open, and show riches
                       Ready to drop upon me; that when I waked,
                       I cried to dream again.

>*Vocal sounds like a haunting melodic cry. The music builds to a climax of sound.*

>BEN *and* ZOE *sit together on the sand. A storm is brewing out at sea. Sounds of thunder mingle with the sound of the waves and the distant music from the rave. There's a loud rumble of thunder.*

ZOE: God, that'd wake the dead. (*To the sky*) Send 'er down, Hughie.

BEN: Hey, knock it off. If it rains Fergus'll be spewin'.

ZOE: No, it'd be choice! We could have a rain dance!

BEN: Hey, yeah. A rave rain dance...

ZOE:... with the whole tribe!

>*They give a joyous tribal yell.*

BEN: I am the spirit of the rain. I'm rising up out of the sea and evaporating into the sky. Into clouds. Then the clouds open... and pow!

ZOE: You piss down on everyone who gives you the shits. (*Brief pause.*) Hey the moon's going behind a cloud.

BEN: The moon was a ghostly galleon...

ZOE: I love it when it does that. (*Brief pause.*) It's coming out again.

BEN: Hello, moon. Hey, watch out! It's falling. It's falling! Aahhhhhh!

> BEN *tries to hug* ZOE.

ZOE: Get stuffed. You're off your face.

> BEN *brings out a packet of jelly snakes from his backpack and offers them to* ZOE.

BEN: Wanna snake?

ZOE: Thanks.

> As ZOE *goes to take one...*

BEN: Oh no! It's Satan! It's Satan! Sssssssss. Want a nice shiny juicy apple from my tree, little girl?

ZOE: God, you're a dag.

> ZOE *eats her snake.*

BEN: Are you seeing anyone at the moment?

ZOE: Nuh. I don't have time for all that. What about you?

BEN: I was. We broke up. Well, she broke up with me.

ZOE: Why?

BEN: She told me I was... emotionally unavailable.

ZOE: Is that the way she talked? Emotionally unavailable. Shit.

BEN: Wouldn't it be amazing if you had someone who loved you no matter what?

ZOE: Unconditional love. Not many people are capable of that.

BEN: No. Tough love, now that's another story.

ZOE: What's that?

BEN: Ask Mum.

> FERGUS *enters with* JENNA. JENNA *is dressed as Ariel.* FERGUS *is Prospero. For a moment they are unaware of* BEN *and* ZOE.

JENNA: Who is she? One of your band of adoring followers?

FERGUS: Careful, babe. Your paranoia's showing again.

JENNA: Who is she, Fergus?

FERGUS: She's been hanging around me for ages. I don't encourage her.

JENNA: It didn't look like that to me. Where'd you find her... in a cereal packet?

FERGUS: Yeah, same place I found you. A packet of Fruit Loops.

JENNA: You're such a slut.

> BEN *and* ZOE *silently begin to creep up on* JENNA *and* FERGUS.

FERGUS: Jenna, you know what some of these chicks are like. They won't leave me alone.

JENNA: Because you are so hot, man.

FERGUS: Shit.

JENNA: Flavour of the month, is she?

FERGUS: You went to Sydney. What was I supposed to do? Live like a fucking priest?

> BEN *and* ZOE *take* FERGUS *and* JENNA *by surprise.*

BEN: Hey, check you guys out.

ZOE: Wow, you look amazing, Jenna. Fab cozzie.

JENNA: He got it for me.

ZOE: You're supposed to be some kind of bug, right?

JENNA: (*mirthlessly*) You lose. (*Wheel of Fortune sound effects:*) Wah, wah, wah, wah.

ZOE: A bull-ant?

FERGUS: I think your... Ariel needs adjusting?

ZOE: Nuh. Don't get it.

FERGUS: She's Ariel. I'm Prospero.

ZOE: What?

FERGUS: Rave New World? *The Tempest*? Shakespeare? I'm the magician. She's under my spell. Watch. Approach, my Ariel, come!

> FERGUS *gestures hypnotically.* JENNA *goes to* FERGUS. *He puts his arms around her.*

See? My art is of such power.

> BEN *tries the same routine on* ZOE.

BEN: Approach, my Zoe, come!

ZOE: Get fucked! So what's this Ariel thing? Are you supposed to be his slave or something?

JENNA: Yeah.

ZOE: Why?

JENNA: It's just a game.

ZOE: His slave. I couldn't stand that.

JENNA: It's a game, okay? (*To* FERGUS) I'm not his fucking slave.

FERGUS: Why, that's my dainty Ariel. I shall miss thee, but yet thou shalt have freedom.

JENNA: You're so full of shit sometimes, Fergus.

FERGUS: Come on, Jenn... let's go back and dance.

> FERGUS *goes to leave.* JENNA *doesn't follow.* FERGUS *gestures dramatically.*

FERGUS: Jenna!

JENNA: Nuh. I don't want to.

> ZOE *laughs.*

FERGUS: Jenna. Come on, babe. Let's go.

JENNA: You always have to be in control.

FERGUS: Sorry about this, guys.

JENNA: You think if you mooned at the ocean the tide would come in.

FERGUS: Hey, come on. Be nice.

JENNA: Why should I? You couldn't give a shit about me.

FERGUS: You know that's not true.

JENNA: Do I?

FERGUS: Jenna, knock it off.

JENNA: Do you love me, Fergus?

FERGUS: Yeah.

JENNA: Say it.

FERGUS: I fucking love you. Now come on...

JENNA: Let's prove it. Ben...

> FERGUS *takes hold of* JENNA.

FERGUS: Hey, Jenna. Cool it.

JENNA: Fuck off. Ben...

FERGUS: Jenna. I said cool it. Okay, babe?

JENNA: Leave me alone.

FERGUS: Jenna. This is really starting to piss me off.

JENNA: I want to talk to Ben.

FERGUS: This is not the time.

JENNA: Let go. I'm talking to him.

FERGUS: This is a party. Jenna? This is a party. Don't do this.

JENNA: Fuck off!

FERGUS: Jenna. Keep it nice or you go. You go. Okay?

JENNA: I'm not your slave anymore, remember?

> JENNA *takes off her Ariel crown and throws it at* FERGUS*'feet.*

FERGUS: She's in hobbit land, man. Dead set cuckoo world.

JENNA: (*trying to pull away*) Don't.

> *Again* FERGUS *tries to remove* JENNA. *He is more rough this time.* ZOE *and* BEN *notice.*

ZOE: Hey, pull your head in, Fergus.

BEN: Fergus... hey, man.

FERGUS: Jenna, he doesn't want to hear this now.

JENNA: The night Stacy died...

FERGUS: Jenna!

BEN: Let her go.

> FERGUS *releases* JENNA.

JENNA: The night Stacy died, I'd gone to Fergus's place to get some stuff...

FERGUS: Shit.

JENNA: I was hoping we could spend some time together. But when I got there, there was someone with him. It was Stacy, and they'd been...

FERGUS: (*cutting in*) Okay, look. This is what happened, okay? She'd turned up at my place in a really bad way. She said her mother had pissed her off. She was hysterical. Crying her eyes out.

BEN: Why didn't you tell me this, man?

JENNA: She went to you because she trusted you. And you screwed her.

BEN: What?

FERGUS: Oh, man, it's not like that.

BEN: What's she telling me, Fergus?

FERGUS: Ben, just...

BEN: You fucked her?

FERGUS: She came to me, man.

BEN: You fucked her!

FERGUS: Ben! Just shut up and listen, all right? Stacy really wanted some stuff. She said she needed some e but she didn't have any cash. So I said, just joking, what's it worth? And the next minute she's all over me. Like I said, your mum had told her to piss off and she was really cut. She needed someone to hold her, you know? To give her a bit of loving. And she was really hanging out for that ekkie, man. If she hadn't got it from me she would have got it somewhere else. What do you want me to tell you? That I let her go and get it from some fuck-wit off the street? You know what some of that shit's like. They cut it with any kind of crap. And I had some very good tabs...

JENNA: Fergus and I were arguing. The next minute Stacy starts spewing everywhere. She was really trashed. I asked Fergus what she'd had, and he said a few e's and some bourbon.

FERGUS: Hey. I didn't *give* her the bourbon, man. No way. I turn my back for a minute and the next thing I know she's she getting stuck into my booze. I didn't give her bourbon. Not on top of the ekkies. I'm not a fucking idiot.

JENNA: I told him she'd already done a heap of shit that afternoon...

FERGUS: I didn't know about that either...

JENNA:... and that she'd had too much.

FERGUS: So what did I do, Jenna? I got some wet washers and I put them all over her...

JENNA: And then he goes... serves you right, you little drug guts.

FERGUS: Bullshit! I didn't say that!

JENNA: Stacy looked bad. She's shivering but she's really sweating, you know? And he starts to panic. He had this important gig to go to and he was running late. So he says... call Ben. Tell him you'll bring Stacy to the club. And make sure you don't mention me. What he doesn't know won't hurt him.

FERGUS: That's crap.

JENNA: So we put her in the van and brought her to the Crystal. It was pretty crowded, but after a while we saw you.

FERGUS: Yeah, see? You were there, so no worries.

JENNA: And Fergus goes... don't tell Ben you were with me, Stace. He wouldn't like it. Then he looks at me and he says... are you staying with her or coming with me? So I said... there's Ben, Stace.

He'll look after you. Go to Ben. (*Brief pause.*) As we left, she was walking towards you.

FERGUS: She was just fine. Wasn't she, Jenn? When we left she was...

JENNA: She was off her face.

SCENE SIXTEEN

Change of lighting state. The Crystal. The music swells up. STACY *is walking towards* BEN. *She hugs him.* BEN *immediately realises that* STACY *is in trouble. He takes her out onto the fire escape.*

STACY: Hey, Benny.

BEN: Stace...

STACY: You're here. I knew you would be.

BEN: Shit.

STACY: You'll look after me.

BEN: Have you been with Jenna?

STACY: Jenny, Jenn, Jenna...

BEN: Where is she?

> STACY *sways giddily.* BEN *grabs her.*

BEN: What did she give you?

STACY: Who?

BEN: Jenna. What did she give you, Stacy?

STACY: Let me go back in. I wanna dance.

BEN: (*shaking her*) Stacy. How much stuff have you had?

STACY: Dunno.

BEN: Shit. I'll kill her.

STACY: You're wonderful.

BEN: You're coming home.

> STACY *wraps her arms around* BEN *and hugs him again.*

STACY: I love you. You're lovely.

BEN: Mum wants you to come home.

STACY: Yeah, right.

BEN: She does, Stace. All you have to do is stop trashing yourself with all this shit.

STACY: Nope. Don't wanna.

BEN: Come on. I'm taking you home, now.
STACY: No. Piss off! Leave me alone. I want to dance.
BEN: Stacy.

> STACY *struggles away from* BEN *and escapes back inside the club.* BEN *follows her. The music and drumming become wilder.* STACY *tries to hurl herself into the frenzied beat. There is no sense of ecstasy this time.*

> STACY *stands swaying for a moment, clenching and unclenching her fists. She then collapses to the floor.* BEN *rushes forward to catch her. He sinks to the floor with her.*

BEN: It's okay. I've got you.
STACY: I can't feel my hands.
BEN: What?
STACY: I can't feel my hands.
BEN: Shit.
STACY: I'm frightened.
BEN: Sshhh. You'll be all right.
STACY: I'm scared, Ben.
BEN: No, don't be. I'm here.
STACY: So, I'll be all right.
BEN: Yes.

> BEN *holds* STACY. *Suddenly she becomes very sick. Dry retching.*

STACY: Sorry. Sorry.
BEN: It's okay.

> BEN *tries to lift her up. She is sick again.*

STACY: I don't like this. Make it stop.

> STACY*'s eyes roll back. She collapses. Again* BEN *tries to lift her. She is a dead weight.*

BEN: Hey, Stace!

> STACY *opens her eyes for a moment and stares at* BEN *seemingly without recognition.* BEN *cradles her helplessly.*

Stacy? Come on, mate. Shit. Oh, shit.

He looks around desperately. The music builds. The shadowy dancers swirl around them.

BEN: Hey! Can someone please help me? There's somebody very sick here...

The music builds. BEN *continues to call to the other dancers.*

BEN: Help me someone. I don't know what to do. Somebody? Help me! I need help here! Jesus!

SCENE SEVENTEEN

Lighting change. The beach. Light focused on BEN *spreads out again to reveal* JENNA, FERGUS *and* ZOE. JENNA*'s words are continuing...*

JENNA:... and that night, when you phoned from the hospital to ask where I was, he told you he hadn't seen me. But I was standing right beside him. We both could have told you what she'd taken that night...

FERGUS: (*quietly*) Fuck.

JENNA:... but he told me to shut up, because if any of it got out, it'd ruin his chances of becoming this big shot DJ. And he promised we'd go away together and live happily ever after. So I said yes. I said yes to everything because basically I agreed that my shithouse life was worth fuck-all without him. (*Momentary pause.*) So. Do you still love me, Fergus?

A silence.

BEN: I needed to know what she'd taken. I needed to know what fucking drugs she'd taken!

FERGUS: How was I to know she was going to screw up? Some can handle it, some can't. You know that. Anyway, you gave her stuff. (*To* JENNA) So did you. Were you forcing it on her? (*To* BEN) Were you? No fucking way. It's supply and demand. People make their own choices. I didn't force it on her. I didn't force anything on her. I know you think she was all the angels and saints rolled into one, but let me tell you, she wasn't. She was... she was the one who screwed up, not me. Not me. How was I supposed to know she was going to fucking die? (*confronting* JENNA) You just fucked yourself, babe. Let's see how long you last in the real world. (*Brief pause.*) Fuck this! Fuck this! Fuck youse. Do what you fucking want. I'm out of here.

FERGUS *exits. After a moment* ZOE *goes to* BEN.

ZOE: Ben?

BEN: It's all crap, isn't it? All this.

ZOE: What?

BEN: This scene. All the peace, love, unit and respect bullshit.

ZOE: He's not the scene. He's only one person.

BEN: It's all fake.

ZOE: Yeah, course it is. So?

A pause.

BEN: When Stacy got sick that night, I brought her back to her own room. I didn't wake Mum. I knew she wouldn't have been able to handle it, seeing Stacy like that. There was spew on the sheets. In her hair. I just sat with her, watching her, holding her hand. Willing her to get better. I even invited God to help, but he must have been busy that day. (*Brief pause.*) About five o'clock in the morning I woke Mum. We called an ambulance and got her to hospital. Then we just waited. Finally they said we could see her. She was hooked up to all these machines and tubes and crap. She didn't look like Stace anymore. But she was alive, and she seemed to be hanging in there, you know? And for a while we thought she might make it. But then they told us no. She wouldn't. Her brain's totally fucked. Stacy's brain dead and she's going to die.

A pause.

Then Mum had to decide whether she was going to be cut up and her organs donated to... whatever. It's the old supply and demand see.

A pause.

I should have got help straight away. I should have called the ambulance. But I was shit scared. She's done all this stuff, see, and I thought they'd call the cops...

ZOE: They wouldn't...

BEN: I know. I know that now, don't I? I'm sorry. I'm so sorry. I didn't know what to do! Jesus Christ. Can't you understand that? I didn't know what to fucking do.

ZOE: You did what you thought was right.

JENNA: You loved her, Ben.

BEN: Oh, yeah. I loved her to death.

> *A pause.*

I feel so... angry. At her. It was so stupid, what she did. I hate her for it.

> BEN *breaks down.* JENNA *rushes to* BEN *and holds him. They cling to each other. The music swells up and carries over into the next scene.*

SCENE EIGHTEEN

Lighting change. ANNE *is trying to distract herself with housework, but she is obviously worried. She checks her watch.* BEN *and* ZOE *enter.*

ANNE: Where on earth were you?

ZOE: At the rave.

ANNE: I was getting so worried. I thought you'd be home ages ago.

> *A pause.* ZOE *looks at* BEN.

What's up?

ZOE: There's someone outside.

ANNE: Who?

BEN: We've got someone with us.

ANNE: Who is it?

ZOE: Jenna.

ANNE: Jenna.

ZOE: Is it alright if she stays here for a couple of nights? She could just crash in my room. There's plenty of space.

ANNE: What's going on Ben?

BEN: She's out on her arse, Mum. She's got nowhere to stay.

ZOE: It'd just be for a night or two.

ANNE: (*to* BEN) You want her here?

BEN: She's got nowhere else.

ANNE: In this house?
BEN: Mum...
ANNE: I'm sorry. I can't.

> ANNE *returns to her work.* BEN *turns abruptly and begins to walk away.*

Ben. Wait a moment. (*Brief pause.*) I don't understand.
BEN: Mum... it's all right.
ANNE: Is it?
BEN: Yes.

> *Brief pause.*

ANNE: I don't know if I've got many spare pillows.
ZOE: We'll manage.
ANNE: (*to* BEN) You think it's all right?
BEN: Yes.
ANNE: Where is she?
ZOE: Waiting down the bus stop. She wouldn't come near the house until we'd spoken to you.

> *A pause.* ZOE *exits.*

ANNE: I really hate this, Ben.
BEN: What?
ANNE: I hate it when you spring things on me. Why do you always do that?
BEN: Me? Spring things on you? Yeah, right, Mum.

> BEN *sees the Smurf resting against a chair. He goes to it and picks it up.*

Remember when she got this fella?
ANNE: Yes.
BEN: Old Boofhead.
ANNE: You bought it for her fourteenth birthday.
BEN: Stupid bloody thing.
ANNE: She was a great one for the toys.
BEN: Yeah. She never did grow up.
ANNE: No.

> *A pause.*

Some of the people down at church, they keep saying... she's gone to a better place. They say this old world's certainly not much chop, is it, the way things are. But I think if she'd had a choice she would have preferred to stay. I mean, she loved that old Boofhead for a start.

BEN: Yeah. (*Momentary pause.*) And she loved to eat. She was a real garbage guts.

ANNE: She was good on the tooth all right.

BEN: She hated you saying that.

ANNE: She did.

BEN: Crappy tomato sauce on bloody everything.

ANNE: Yeah.

    A pause.

Do you remember when she was really little, she couldn't have been more than seven, we took you kids to see the Light Parade at Expo? We pushed you both right to the front of the crowd so you could see.

BEN: Yeah. That was an excellent night.

ANNE: Remember all those people in gorgeous costumes, all draped with lights?

BEN: Yeah.

ANNE: They looked like creatures from another world, all shimmering. And one of them, some sort of... fairy thing she was, she came out of the parade and touched Stacy with her wand, as if she were granting her a wish. I remember thinking it was like some kind of... good omen for her whole life. (*Brief pause.*) I really miss her, don't you?

BEN: Stacy? Nah. Shit no. She was a pain in the arse.

    ANNE *smiles at* BEN.

Mum. I'm sorry.

ANNE: For what?

BEN: For what? What do you think?

    ANNE *begins to walk away from* BEN.

ANNE: Ben, this really isn't a good time for me now. I've got this presentation...

BEN: Well now's a good time for me. Now's a fucking good time for me.

ANNE: Please don't speak to me like that.

BEN: Jesus, Mum. Please don't do this. Don't shut me out again! It makes me feel like I'm dead as well. Talk to me! Talk to me, for Christ's sake. I screwed up, okay? I didn't get her to the hospital. I'm sorry. I'm sorry. I don't know what else to say to you.

Brief pause.

ANNE: Would you like a cup of tea?

BEN: Mum?

ANNE: (*breaking*) I'm sorry. I'm so sorry. I pushed her away. The last words she heard from me were so angry. And I don't understand why. I don't understand anything any more.

BEN *goes quickly to* ANNE *and holds her.*

BEN: Mum, it's okay...

ANNE: After she died, I'd go into her room and lie down on her bed. I'd bury my face in her pillow. I could still breathe in the smell of her. Sometimes it was like I was actually holding her in my arms. (*Brief pause.*) Do you want to hear something really silly? The other night, I dreamt she was back. She was sitting right here. My beautiful girl. I said... I thought you were dead. And she said... as if. She was... it was so real.

ANNE *touches* BEN*'s face.*

ANNE: Ben...

BEN: Yeah. It's okay. I know.

ZOE *enters.*

ZOE: Jenna's here.

JENNA *enters tentatively.*

ANNE: Hello, love. Come in...

SCENE NINETEEN

Lighting change. Music swells up. Segue into the university lecture room. ANNE *is delivering her Signs and Meanings lecture to a group of students (the audience). She is showing an overhead projection of St Teresa of Avila.*

ANNE: I think that what Bernini was trying to do when he created this sculpture was to show that in the moment of ecstasy, opposites are united. And all feelings of joy and sorrow, pleasure and pain, good and evil, innocence and guilt become as one. (*Brief pause.*) Teresa came back into the world, and strongly into the world. Some don't come back. And they're lost to us.

SCENE TWENTY

The Crystal. Lights and music. Cheers and whistles. DJ ZOE-E*'s voice over music. 'Now my charms are all o'erthrown, and what strength I have's my own.'*

Lights slowly down.

THE END

Teacher's Notes

written & compiled by Helen Radvan*

INTRODUCTION

I hope you find these Teacher's Notes helpful in assisting you prepare your students for assessing the play and for finding ways to approach the complex issues raised.

As writer of these notes, I clearly acknowledge the sensitivity required for classroom discussion with students concerning the issues and themes contained in the play, which will undoubtedly strike strong resonances with some students and their parents and teachers. For this reason I strongly recommend Drama teachers seek the expert guidance of school support staff (Life Skills/Human Relationship Education teachers, Health Education teachers, School Guidance or Religious Counsellors) who may be able to assist in preparing study material and to provide relevant additional resource material.

X-Stacy is a play every senior high school student should read. Considerable time may be needed to unpack the messages it contains. It is a challenging, confronting and compassionate play which deals with different relationships in crisis. As director Sue Rider has stated, *X-Stacy* is not 'an education program, nor a documentary, but a play'.

X-Stacy explores, with honesty and insight, the confusions, misunderstandings and depth of feeling experienced by young people and their parents as they struggle to come to terms with a tragedy that has disturbed their lives and challenged their faith. It is an important play for young people to read and to share with the adult figures in their lives such as parents and teachers.

---

*   The writer acknowledges contributions of ideas, resources and feedback by Lowanna Dunn (QUT), Margery Forde, Jane Klease (Lifeskills Teacher, Wellington Point SHS), Anne Lawson (Wellington Point SHS), Bernadette Pryde (Freelance Teacher), Mark Radvan (QUT) and Debbie Wall (Queensland Arts Council).

Drama students in particular will be able to identify how the playwright has cleverly structured the play, utilising the elements of drama to communicate her messages more effectively and to drive the dramatic action more intensely. It is an excellent play to focus on in an Australian Drama Unit, a Theatre for Young People Unit, a Drama for Social Action Unit, an Issues-Based Drama Unit or even a Unit that specifically studies Dramatic Elements, Form and Style (e.g., Playwriting).

Considering the critical issue of teenage illicit drug use and teenage death-related drug use, this is a play that speaks to any young person, regardless of whether or not they study Drama, and affirms the important role theatre can play in our lives.

BIOGRAPHY OF THE PLAYWRIGHT

Margery Forde began her writing life as a copywriter with radio station 4BH, Brisbane. She has written numerous productions for mainhouse theatre, community theatre and theatre for young people. Her writing credits include *My Life is Love*, *Ghosts of Something Irish*, *1901*, *Knock 'em Dead* and *Snapshots from Home*, for which she received a 1996 AWGIE Award from the Australian Writers' Guild. As documenter on workshops about sexuality and the aged (a joint project with Queensland Performing Arts Trust and the Ethnic Communities Council), she scripted *What Next?!!*, which was performed at QPAT's Merivale Street Studio, and *What Next 2?!!*, for which she received a 1998 AWGIE Award. She writes scripts for audio and visual productions for the Open Access Support Unit, Education Queensland. In 1997 she received an Award of Commendation in the Lord Mayor's Australia Day Cultural Awards. Margery has also co-written a number of works for the stage with her husband, Michael Forde, including *Milo's Wake*.

THE STORY

Ben goes to dance parties and finds ecstasy in the music, the dancing and the drugs. In her search for ecstasy, his mother, Anne, turns to the writings of a Spanish mystic. When Ben initiates his sister, Stacy, into the world of dance parties, her experience is ecstatic. But gradually Stacy's drug taking spins out of control and she dies from the effects of a drug cocktail. The consequences for Ben and his mother are devastating. The story also looks at the effects of Stacy's death on a group of friends. Out of a plot which deals with miscommunication, manipulation and misdirected loyalties, emerge themes of spiritual fulfilment, negotiating pathways between new moralities and the paradox of loneliness within the tribe.

SYNOPSIS

SCENE ONE

In the dark a recorded message on an answer machine. Ben has called Jenna to ask if she has seen Stacy. Lights up on Anne at Mass. Father Paul is on the altar. Lights down. Lights up on DJ Fergus as he creates the dance party event at the Crystal. The dance party concludes, Ben and Fergus are packing up. Jenna arrives and tries to speak to Ben. She is greeted with silent hostility. Zoe approaches Fergus asking for work as a DJ.

SCENE TWO

A recorded telephone message. Ben has called Fergus, looking for Stacy. It's the Sunday morning after the dance party at the Crystal. Zoe turns up unexpectedly at Ben's home. Ben's mother, Anne, has rented out Stacy's room to Zoe without consulting Ben. Ben is furious. Father Paul arrives to give Anne some books on St Teresa of Avila for her forthcoming university presentation. Zoe discovers a Smurf in her room. She shows it to Ben.

SCENE THREE

Flashback to Stacy's fourteenth birthday. Ben has bought Stacy the Smurf as a present. It's Sunday morning and Stacy tells Ben to get ready for Mass. Ben says he's not going. However, Stacy manipulates the situation when Anne arrives on the scene, and Ben finally does what he's told.

SCENE FOUR

Back to the present. Father Paul and Ben have a stilted conversation. Paul touches on the subject of Stacy, and Ben confides that he and his mother never talk about her. Paul suggests that Ben come to Mass, but Ben says that he's found something more fulfilling, the rave.

SCENE FIVE

A recorded message. Jenna has called Ben and asked him to meet her at the club. She says that Stacy is with her. Anne rehearses her university presentation for Zoe. Anne quizzes Zoe about drugs and dance parties. In her presentation, Anne asks questions about the human desire for the ecstatic state.

SCENE SIX

Anne's phone call to the ambulance. Zoe is excited about her first gig as a DJ at the Crystal. Jenna is also at the Crystal, and Ben confronts her about Stacy. Fergus defuses the situation. Fergus tells Zoe that Ben's made a mistake, and that she's not playing a set after all. Ben is depressed, but Fergus tries to cheer him up by recalling his first DJ gig at the Crystal. Ben remembers that it was also Stacy's first dance party.

SCENE SEVEN

Flashback. Ben initiates Stacy by giving her an ecstasy. Fergus is introduced to the crowd on his first gig at the Crystal. Stacy is flying.

SCENE EIGHT

Back to the present. Ben tries to reconcile with Zoe. He apologises for making a mistake about her playing a set. Zoe questions Ben about Stacy, but Ben volunteers no information. Fergus arrives with tickets to the Rave New World event.

SCENE NINE

A phone call. Ben calls Fergus from the hospital. He tells Fergus that Stacy has done too many drugs, and the doctors need to know what she's taken. Ben wants to speak to Jenna, but Fergus says he hasn't seen her. Saturday evening Mass. Anne is in church. Father Paul asks her to take communion to the sick. Anne confronts Paul. She accuses him of not doing anything to help her when Stacy started doing drugs.

SCENE TEN

Flashback to Stacy being suspended from school after smoking pot. Stacy's remorse and Anne's confusion at the discovery.

SCENE ELEVEN

Ben arrives home from the club to find Anne studying. He accuses her of 'keeping vigil'. Anne confronts Ben about his drug taking. He tries to express how he is feeling, but the doors of communication slam shut. Ben turns on his CD player and closes his eyes.

SCENE TWELVE

Flashback to Stacy and Jenna at home. They are smoking pot from a bong. Ben tells Stacy she's already been warned and pleads with her to get rid of the bong before Anne comes home. Anne arrives home early from work. There's a bitter confrontation and Anne throws Stacy out. Ben and Anne are left alone.

SCENE THIRTEEN

Back to the present. Ben is listening to music. Zoe demands that he turns it down. There is an argument and accusations. Ben invites Zoe to come with him to the Rave New World.

SCENE FOURTEEN

Sunday morning after Mass. Anne goes to Paul and tells him that she can't take communion to the sick. She asks Paul why she should keep her faith after all that has happened to her. Anne says goodbye to Paul.

SCENE FIFTEEN

The Rave New World event. There is music and ecstatic dancing. Zoe and Ben chill out on the beach as a storm is brewing. Fergus and Jenna enter. They are arguing, and are surprised by Ben and Zoe. Ignoring protests from Fergus, Jenna finally reveals the story of the night of Stacy's death. As Jenna tells her story, Ben recalls what happened at the Crystal on the night Stacy died.

SCENE SIXTEEN

Flashback. Ben has gone to the club to meet Jenna and Stacy. Stacy is there alone. She becomes violently ill on the dance floor. Ben feels helpless and panic stricken. Nobody will come to his assistance.

SCENE SEVENTEEN

The present. Jenna is continuing her story. She tells Ben that when he rang from the hospital to talk to Fergus, she was there with him. They both could have told him what Stacy had taken that night. Fergus ferociously tries to defend his actions. He goes… leaving Ben, Zoe and Jenna alone on the beach. Ben reveals his story about not getting Stacy to the hospital in time.

SCENE EIGHTEEN

Ben and Zoe return from the Rave New World. They ask Anne if Jenna can stay for a few nights. Anne is stunned. Zoe leaves Ben and Anne alone. Ben finds the Smurf, and they begin to talk about Stacy. Then Anne shuts Ben out again. Ben pleads with her to talk to him, and finally Anne breaks. Ben and Anne are at last able to share their grief. Zoe returns with Jenna. Anne invites her in.

SCENE NINETEEN

Anne delivers the final part of her presentation on The Ecstasy of St Teresa to a university audience.

SCENE TWENTY

DJ Zoe's voice over music: *'Now my charms are all o'er thrown, and what strength I have's my own.'*

SEQUENCING ACTIVITIES

Margery Forde has written a play which is interesting in its structure, form and style. The use of flashbacks is a dramatic technique which helps to heighten the emotional impact of the piece, intensifying the dramatic action and helps the audience to make sense of the events leading up to the tragic death of the character Stacy. It also assists the audience to gain an insight into different characters' consciences and helps to establish the identity of the deceased character—Stacy.

1. IDENTIFYING KEY MOMENTS USING TABLEAUX

The teacher can run through the detailed synopsis of the play with students. Students working in small groups, or as a whole class, can then capture the main action of each scene using frozen tableaux to assist in recalling the progressive action of the play. A further option would be to have the students accompany each tableau with a key word that best sums up the main mood of each scene, e.g., Scene One could be *anticipation*. Students can then discuss the range of moods contained in the play and why they thought the playwright chose to convey those different moods throughout the piece.

2. ANALYSING STRUCTURE AND STYLE

I suppose you'd call it naturalism, but it's heightened naturalism. A playwright is constantly trying to find ways of bringing human truths to the stage, but to do it in a heightened form... And the structure of the story isn't linear. We keep taking jumps backward in time. Through Ben's memories, we re-live parts of Stacy's life leading up to the night of her death.

Margery Forde (Playwright)

Students are asked to consider and discuss the structure and style of the play, using the detailed synopsis provided and reading the playwright's comments above. Students should comment further on the playwright's decision to incorporate the use of flashbacks. How effective are they? How do they help contribute to the overall meaning of the piece?

3. PLOTTING THE DRAMATIC STRUCTURE OF THE PLAY AND IDENTIFYING THE ELEMENT OF DRAMATIC TENSION

Using butcher's paper, students can plot out the dramatic structure of the play, scene by scene, in graph structure. They should consider the elements of dramatic structure including Introduction, Inciting Action, Rising Action, Climax/Catastrophe, Falling Action and Resolution. The teacher can also use this graph to discuss how the element of tension was incorporated throughout the play and the different types of tension that existed. These tensions can also be plotted on the graph.

SETTING

It is important to knit all themes together seamlessly. The mother's search for meaning through the Roman Catholic Faith; the pseudo-religious imagery and atmosphere of dance parties; religion and drugs as vehicles to escape; and 'consciousness'.

Dance parties are sometimes held in abandoned or unused buildings. So a deconsecrated church seemed like a good venue to place the two spheres of action. I needed to incorporate house interiors and the 'chill-out' area of a dance party whilst also providing a 'place' to put furniture.

Costumes are modern and, therefore, not really designed, but rather co-ordinated.

The only two costume 'design' considerations are Ariel, a sort of Space-Age Fairy, and the DJ and Priest, who I wanted to make similar in style. They are played by the same actor, and, in some ways, they are the same character—the Father divine, and the adored and revered DJ.

Kate Stewart (Designer of the original stage production)

SETTING ACTIVITIES

1. SETTING COLLAGE

Using magazines and drawings, students can create a collage of images that depict the two main settings of the play—the church and the dance party. A discussion can follow which focuses on the similarities and differences of these two settings. Students should consider elements such as contrast, colour, symbols, etc.

2. COLLECTIVE DRAWING—ESTABLISHING A SENSE OF PLACE—SETTING

For this exercise, the teacher places large sheets of butcher's paper and pens around different locations within the classroom. On each paper is the name of one setting from the play. This activity involves students working either individually or in small groups, rotating around the room and drawing a collective picture in as much or as little detail as possible. Their contributions should reflect their shared response to, or understanding of, that particular place which is established in the play. The pictures can be supplemented with statements that give more detail and express feelings, thoughts or opinions held about the different places. They may just like to contribute adjectives which help them describe the feelings associated with these different places:

> An old disused warehouse
> Roman Catholic Church
> A 19/20-year-old boy's bedroom
> Inside the Crystal—a dance party club
> Catholic family living room
> Outside the Crystal
> A 14-year-old girl's bedroom
> A dance party event at a beach
> A university lecture room

After the exercise is carried out, the drawings are discussed with the focus being on how different places within the play may hold different meanings and associations for different characters and the audience.

3. DEFINING VARIOUS SETTINGS

Using available furniture and material, students working in small groups, or as a whole class, are to try to 'accurately' represent and define the different locations/settings of the play. These locations are provided in the above activity. After each location is established, students can also position themselves or others in the space.

Following this activity students are to then find a way of rearranging the furniture, etc. into a single configuration so that the space can be used for any or all of the settings with little or no changes needed.

4. ATMOSPHERE ACTIVITY ESTABLISHING THE ELEMENTS OF MOOD AND SPACE/PLACE

The teacher calls out to the class one of the given locations within the play. See above list (2).

Selected students, one by one, are to enter the space. Their entry into the space should help to show the audience exactly where they are, e.g., Church. They may like to mime some simple actions, e.g., praying, taking communion, singing, reading, listening, preaching, etc. to help clarify exactly where they are. They are also to consider what type of mood would be associated with that particular place and try to establish that mood.

Colour association could also be helpful for investigating and expressing different moods. Considering the different settings within the play, students could brainstorm the colours associated with those places. For example: Church—white, reds, browns, stained glass, etc.

5. SOUND TRACKING—CREATING ATMOSPHERE AND IDENTIFYING MOOD

This activity can immediately follow the collective drawing activity, or the above element of space/place activity, or it can be used on its own as a separate activity. Students working in small groups, or as a whole group, are to create a soundscape which helps to create the atmosphere of a selected setting where the action of the play takes place.

Students can also draw upon the different types of interactions that take place within the given setting and try to incorporate, in sounds, the mood created in that specific setting by the characters. For example, the interaction occurring between Fergus and Ben at the Crystal is very different from the interaction occurring between Ben and his mother, Anne, at their family home.

Students can use pre-recorded sounds, music, instruments, fragmented dialogue, or if such resources are unavailable, just the sounds of their own voices incorporating vocal dynamics, repetition, etc. The sounds should be a combination of the realistic and the stylised.

6. DISCUSS THE PLAYWRIGHT'S CHOICE OF SETTINGS

Students can make a list of the reasons why the playwright has chosen these main two contrasting settings of a dance party club and a Roman Catholic church, and can then discuss in what ways both settings have helped contribute to the overall meaning and themes of the play.

7. DESIGNING TASK

Students are given the task to design a poster or a flyer that would advertise and/or promote this play. What images would students choose? Why?

THEMES AND ISSUES

GRIEF AND LOSS

The story of X-Stacy *in a line? Stacy dies from drugs, and those who loved her must deal with their grief.*

Margery Forde

In the play, *X-Stacy*, the characters have experienced loss and are at different stages of grieving. The action of the play takes place nine months after the death of Stacy occurs. All characters in the play are, to various extents, searching for reasons why the loss occured and are tormenting themselves with how they, themselves, could have prevented her death. Most characters in the play are also tormented by their own sense of guilt, feeling the weight of their own actions having impacted upon and contributed towards the tragic death. The result of such intense and heightened states of emotion produces inner conflict and breakdowns in communication amongst the central characters.

> ANNE: No. She's dead. That's it. She's gone. There are times when it just catches me by surprise, you know? It's like someone has their fist pressing here. Pressing really hard. Pressing so hard I can barely breathe.

(Scene Fourteen, pg. 48)

STAGES OF GRIEVING

The process of adjusting to the loss of someone, or grieving, has variously been described by psychologists and psychiatrists (e.g., Elisabeth Kubler Ross) to include a number of 'stages'. The loss may be of someone or something (e.g., a limb). An individual may go through all the stages, may skip some, may alter the order, or be in several at once. An individual getting stuck in one stage may be a cause for concern.

H. Bauman, in the book *Living Through Grief* (Oxford: Lion Publishing, 1978), identifies this process of accepting loss in six stages. Bauman believes that it is important to express your grief for something (or someone) that you have lost in order for you to accept that it has happened—that this loss has become a real and definite stage in your life. As a result, you may be able to understand the feelings that you are experiencing and can begin to rebuild the future direction of your life.

Following are the six stages that Bauman identifies.

THE SIX STAGES OF GRIEF AND LOSS ACCORDING TO BAUMAN:

1. **Shock.** Someone in sudden grief may have feelings of revolt, of not understanding. As a result they may go into shock.
2. **Numbness / Denial.** In the second stage of grief a person may feel as though s/he is partially anaesthetised. Things do not seem real. Everything becomes a daze and s/he is not able to think clearly. His/Her actions seem surreal and s/he may try to convince himself/herself that the death didn't *really* occur.
3. **Fantasy and Guilt.** As a consequence of the shock, a person may feel that s/he is finding life a struggle between fantasy and reality. A person may try to understand where the lost one is or what they went through when dying. S/he may ask questions like 'what if' and 'if only'. These questions can stir up guilty feelings. These feelings of guilt may cause the development of a fantasy world, particularly if there were feelings of resentment or issues that were unresolved with that person. S/he may also feel as though s/he has betrayed that person simply by living, by being the one that is still alive.
4. **Release of Grief.** This is when the person moves towards accepting the reality of the loss. While this reaction may be delayed for some time, it is usually strong. Reactions can range from tears to violence.

5. **Painful Memories.** When someone dies it is tempting to cherish only the best memories of that person. It is important that less-than-happy memories are remembered along with the pleasant ones. Thus, our thoughts of the person are more realistic and truer to his/ her human experience. By remembering exactly who s/he was and who/what we were to him/her, we can accept the pain and begin to re-adjust to living without the person.

6. **Learning to Live Again.** This stage is about reaffirming life. When the loss is accepted, the grief has been spent, and the memories have been dealt with, it is then that we can experience a new life. Acknowledging and accepting this reality is a doorway to new life.

ACTIVITIES

1. SHARING GRIEF AND LOSS EXPERIENCES

Form small groups.

a. In pairs, students share at least one experience which caused grief to someone they know, e.g., loss of a relationship/ friendship, leaving home, a death, etc.
   They should try to describe what happened.

b. Students list at least five feelings which occurred during the grief accompanying the experience.

c. Pairs then report back to the larger group.
   The teacher lists the feelings on the board.

d. Working in small groups, students represent these different grief experiences using tableaux.

e. After the class sharing, students return to small groups and make up a definition of grief. Small groups then report to the class.

2. EXAMPLES OF LOSSES

Students can look at the following table of examples of losses and can brainstorm further examples to add:

I have lost my job	Someone has stolen my savings
I have failed my exams	My parents are going to divorce
I have been turned out of my home	My sister has been accused of shoplifting

I will never walk again	I have been in a motorcycle accident and I am going to lose my leg
My father has left us	I have been dropped from the soccer team
My mother has been diagnosed with cancer	We don't have enough money to see a movie

3. MATCHING ACTIVITY REQUIRING SKILLS IN SCRIPT ANALYSIS

Provided below is a list of scenes from the play which deal with the main characters' grieving states. Students are to try and match the selected quotes spoken by certain characters with the appropriate 'stage' of grieving for each character concerned, according to Bauman. Students need to be able to justify their choices drawing upon key moments in the play to support their ideas.

For example, in the edited extract below the character Zoe, who is unaware of the history surrounding Stacy's absence, questions Ben on Stacy's whereabouts. Instead of admitting to Zoe that Stacy is dead, Ben leaves Zoe with the suggestion that Stacy has simply '*shot through*'. Ben seems to simply dismiss the subject. According to Bauman, Ben would be moving through the second stage of grief here, where he experiences periods of denial.

ZOE: Is that your sister's room?
BEN: Yeah.
ZOE: Where is she?
BEN: Gone to ground.

From the dark, STACY's *voice is heard.*

STACY: Benny, let me in.
ZOE: What, did she shoot through?
BEN: Yeah.

(Scene Two, pg. 13)

Scenes dealing with the issue of grief and loss:

Scene Four, pgs 17–20
Scene Six, pgs 25–27
Scene Eight, pgs 31–32
Scene Nine, pgs 35–37
Scene Eleven, pgs 40–41
Scene Fourteen, pgs 49–50
Scene Seventeen, pgs 59–60
Scene Eighteen, pgs 61–63

4. Use the different grieving stages identified by Bauman (pg. 76 above). Display the list for the students. Explain the concept of a 'journey through' or 'stages of grieving' to other students. Discuss with students that all of us, at different stages in our lives, will grieve. We will also need to support family and friends or partners who are grieving. Use the characters and situations in the play *X-Stacy* to help inform the discussion.

5. Consider the grieving characters in *X-Stacy*. What/Who are they grieving for? How does their grief impact on other characters in the play, i.e., how do other characters in the play support, handle or respond to this character's particular grief?

6. Give small groups a character (you may like to include Stacy) and ask them to identify when in the play they are at different stages of grieving.

7. Ask each group to practise hot seating their character within the group, asking questions of each other to clarify stages of grieving at different points in the play.

8. Create, for example, a 'Ben' journey by asking each of the students who have discussed Ben's character to take a position in the room, freezing in tableau from a moment in the script. The rest of the class visits each 'Ben', asking questions.

RAVES AND RELIGION

As the play focuses on a group of practising Catholics and Ravers in Australia during recent times, it is essential for students to recognise that the different characters' words and actions will be motivated (or at least influenced) by their commitment to the church or the sub-culture. Thus, the language the characters of either group choose to use, how they spend their time, where they feel comfortable and the symbols they recognise all deeply affect the ways in which the characters relate to each other in *X-Stacy*.

While the students could try to follow the story of the play without prior exposure to the Roman Catholic Church or Rave Culture, the characters' dilemmas will be more substantial if students are made aware of the characters' backgrounds and how they are expected to behave in daily life. This awareness, in turn, may allow students to fully sympathise, empathise, condone or challenge the human context that is made explicit on stage.

A glossary has been provided at the end of these notes (pgs 100-103) which offers students and adults alike definitions of key terms associated with religion and youth culture which are often referred to in the play.

BRINGING DRUG CULTURE AND RELIGION TOGETHER THEMATICALLY—IDENTIFYING THE PARALLELS

The DJ is like a high priest on the altar, and he's controlling the music and the dancers.

For many young people, raves and dance parties have a full-on spiritual dimension. They explain it by saying that it comes from the strong feeling of unity and congregation that you get when you're dancing with hundreds, sometimes thousands of other people, all in harmony with each other. Some young people describe it as being a 'transcendental' or 'meditative' experience. One young person that I met at a rave said to me: 'It's like my church coming here. This is my Mass.'

The whole set-up of the rave or dance party has connotations of worship. The DJ is usually placed on a raised platform like an altar, and everyone faces the DJ as they dance. As one young woman expressed it: 'The DJ controls the mass of dancers through the music the way a priest controls a church through prayer.' The music has a base rhythm, a 'doof' that's like a heartbeat, and the DJ controls the music. He or she can bring the dancers up to a peak of excitement, then bring them down again.

Margery Forde

PARALLEL RITUALS

Roman Catholic Church	Rave Culture
Hymns	Techno-music
Seated facing the priest	Dance towards the DJ
Good sermon	Good mix
Achieving communion with God	Achieving trance-like state
Use of special names, e.g., Father Paul	Use of special names, e.g., DJ, Zo-E
Mass	Raves
Communion/Eucharist	Taking ecstasy

PARALLEL ROLES and RELATIONSHIPS

Roman Catholic Church	Rave Culture
Priest	DJ
Congregation	Ravers
Anne and the Priest	Jenna and the DJ
Women are not allowed to be priests	Female DJs get a hard time
The Ten Commandments	Health Promotion and Harm Reduction

PARALLEL SYMBOLS

Roman Catholic Church	Rave Culture
Prayer books	Water bottles
Vestments	DJ gear
Candles, bells	Luminous sticks, whistles
Bible—spreads the word of God	Fliers and ads publicise the Raves
Icons: Holy pictures, crosses, statues, holy medals	Brand name clothes/footwear, accessories, toys (e.g., Smurf)

INFORMATION ON THE CATHOLIC FAITH

The play *X-Stacy* makes mention of Sunday Mass, reveals Catholics attempting to make choices in a modern world, and presents a Catholic family in turmoil. The following information may offer students a general understanding of the Catholic faith so that they can fully appreciate the Catholic characters in the play and the dilemmas and crises they face. It may also offer some insight into the significance of what may otherwise seem like trivial problems to non-Catholics.

Catholics hold certain beliefs which affect the way they think about themselves, other people and the world around them. Their faith has a very strong influence on the way they lead their lives. It has helped to shape their character, their ideals and their values.

The central beliefs of Catholics do not differ from those of other Christians and it's these central beliefs that are at the heart of the Catholic faith, and that most Catholics 'carry round with them'.

The central Catholic beliefs can be summarised like this:

> *God has made himself known and given himself to us in the person of Jesus Christ. Jesus died on the cross to save us from sin and win forgiveness for us. He rose from death and lives on now, through his spirit, in the community of believers which is the Church. As his followers we are to walk in his way by living lives of love and service.*

Catholics use statues, crucifixes and holy pictures as a focus for their prayer to remind them of what Christ has done for mankind, or to bring to mind a saint of the Church whose life is worthy of imitation. They do not pray to statues or pictures and they do not worship them.

> BEN *sees a medal around* STACY*'s neck.*
>
> BEN: What's this?
> STACY: St Teresa of Avila. Sister Laurentia at school gave it to me
> for my birthday.
>
> (Scene Three, pg. 15)

People who know next to nothing about the Catholic Church *do* know *one* thing and that is that Catholics have to go to Mass on Sundays. The majority of Catholics go to Mass on Sundays because they believe it is central to their lives as Christians. The Mass for the majority of Catholics means *Action*. It is something Catholics *do* together. They're not spectators *at it*; they're deeply involved *in it*. The Mass is a sacred action which has a depth of meaning impossible to put into words. As they go to Mass over weeks and months and years, they enter more deeply into its mystery and get more insight into its significance and its meaning for their own lives.

This above reference material was extracted from a book entitled *How to Survive being Married to a Catholic*, Majellan Publications (Brighton, Vic., 1986), Redemptorist Publications.

ACTIVITY—SCRIPT ANALYSIS

In the extracts that follow we see references to aspects of Catholic life and Catholic beliefs. Identify how each person's beliefs are revealed, questioned or challenged. Consider what factors have influenced or impacted upon those beliefs.

EXTRACT 1:

BEN: Now go away. I'm going back to sleep.
STACY: You can't. We've got to go to seven o'clock Mass.
BEN: I'm not going.
STACY: Why?
BEN: Because I'm not.
STACY: Are you sick?
BEN: No.
STACY: You can't just not go.
BEN: Get lost.
STACY: Why aren't you going?
BEN: I don't believe all that crap anymore.
STACY: [*horrified*] What will you say to Mum?
BEN: I'll just tell her.
STACY: She's going to kill you, Ben. She'll absolutely go bonkers.
BEN: Who cares?
STACY: You're going to make trouble on my birthday.
BEN: Tough.

STACY *belts* BEN *with her Smurf.* BEN *fights back.*

STACY: My brother's a big shit.

BEN: Hey. Cut it out!

STACY: Big shitty brother.

BEN: Stacy, drop dead.

STACY: Why did you have to pick today?

> ANNE *enters.*

ANNE: Is the birthday girl in here?

STACY: Ooow!!

ANNE: Hey, careful, Ben. You'll hurt her.

> STACY *runs to her mother and hugs her.*

ANNE: Ben. You're not dressed. Are you sick?

BEN: Nuh.

ANNE: Come on then, love. Up you get.

> BEN *stares moodily at* ANNE.

STACY: Ben. It's my birthday. And it's late. You know how Mum hates walking in late.

> BEN *begins to get out of bed.* ANNE *exits.*

(Scene Three, pgs 16–17)

EXTRACT 2:

PAUL: Goodbye, Ben. Maybe I'll see you at Mass one of these days.

BEN: You reckon? Do you remember the last time I was at Mass?

PAUL: Yes, I do.

> *Brief pause.*

BEN: I've given up on all that.

PAUL: I'm sorry to hear it.

BEN: Don't be.

> *Brief pause.*

PAUL: Say goodbye to your mum for me.

> PAUL *begins to leave.*

BEN: You should come and check out a rave sometime.

PAUL: What was that?

ZOE: He reckons you should come and check out a rave.

PAUL: You think so?

BEN: What I've found there I never found in a church.

PAUL: Is that right?

BEN: Yeah, that's right.

Brief pause.

PAUL: So, what are you finding, Ben?

Brief pause.

BEN: You don't explain it. You feel it.

ZOE *erupts in a giggle.* BEN *glares at her.*

PAUL: Oh. Well, maybe we can talk about it sometime.

No response from BEN.

PAUL: I'll be seeing you.

PAUL *smiles at* ZOE *and exits.*

(Scene Four, pgs 19–20)

EXTRACT 3:

The sacristy of the church. Sounds of organ notes fade away. FATHER PAUL *is taking off his stole and folding it.* ANNE *enters the sacristy.*

ANNE: Father…

PAUL: Hello. I didn't expect to see you this morning. Aren't you supposed to be studying?

ANNE: I can't do this.

PAUL: What?

ANNE: I can't take communion to the sick.

ANNE *hands the pyx to* FATHER PAUL.

ANNE: I'm sorry.

ANNE *begins to exit.* PAUL *stops her gently.*

PAUL: Anne, wait a moment.

ANNE: I've got to get home. I've got this presentation.

PAUL: Tell me what's wrong.

ANNE: I just can't do this anymore. I can't.

Brief pause.

PAUL: Anne, she's in God's hands…

ANNE: No. She's dead. That's it. She's gone. There are times when it just catches me by surprise, you know? It's like someone has their fist pressing here. Pressing really hard. Pressing so hard I can barely breathe.

PAUL: Why don't we just pray gently and… ?

ANNE: Pray to who? All He's ever done is take everything I ever cared about away from me.

PAUL: Anne, listen…

ANNE: Why? There's nothing you can say that will help. Not unless you can make me understand why she went and why I'm losing my son. [*Brief pause.*] You can't.

ANNE *exits.*

(Scene Fourteen, pgs 48–49)

THE ATTRACTION OF RAVES AND DRUG CULTURE

1. The acid/house/rave/techno scene has spanned the globe and snatched the soul of the world's reckless. Apolitical, agnostic and asexual, this particular brand of hedonism has taken modern computers and pharmaceuticals, then plonked them together with dances and beats as old as our species… It's a celebration of house music, of peace, love and tolerance. It's a coming together of the world's youth in a spirit of… togetherness.

The Face Magazine, no. 71, London, August 1994.

2.… Some of my daughter's friends took me to raves and dance parties so I could experience them first hand. And it's not hard to see why they're drawn to it. It's very exciting and tribal. The music's extraordinarily loud, and it comes on like a tidal wave. It pounds up through your feet and into your heart. Every hair on your head feels like it's vibrating with sound. There are hundreds, sometimes thousands of people, all dancing together, and at a certain moment, something will happen in the music, and all the arms raise up together, and there's a great scream or cheer from the dancers. It's thrilling. You get goose bumps.

The philosophy of the rave is 'PLUR'. The philosophy dictates that participants give and receive Peace, Love, Unity and Respect. Young people say that, apart from the music and the dancing, they feel accepted and respected in the scene.

Margery Forde

3. EXTRACT 1:

BEN: You should come and check out a rave sometime.
PAUL: What was that?
ZOE: He reckons you should come and check out a rave.
PAUL: You think so?
BEN: What I've found there I never found in a church.
PAUL: Is that right?
BEN: Yeah, that's right.

Brief pause.

PAUL: So, what are you finding, Ben?

Brief pause.

BEN: You don't explain it. You feel it.

(Scene Four, pg. 19)

4. EXTRACT 2:

ANNE: You go to dance parties?
ZOE: Yeah, course I do. I'm a DJ. Didn't I tell you?
ANNE: No.
ZOE: That's where I met Ben. At the Crystal.
ANNE: And you're telling me you don't take drugs.
ZOE: No way. Dad turned me off doing any of that stuff.
ANNE: Good for him.
ZOE: Heck yeah. He's a real pothead my dad. His whole life revolves around that shit. Got to have his bowl of mull on the table every night or he totally loses it. Abuses the fridge if there's no milk, that kind of crap. Who needs it?

Brief pause.

ANNE: I think Ben does.
ZOE: Does he? I wouldn't know.

Brief pause.

ANNE: If it's not for the drugs, why do you go?

ZOE: Are you kidding? For the music, man. The music's fully excellent. That's what it's all about.

(Scene Five, pg. 22)

ACTIVITY—SCRIPT ANALYSIS

After reading the above depiction of rave culture (1) featured in a popular English magazine, the account of the playwright's experience of raves and dance parties as part of her research (2), and after analysing the two extracts above (3 & 4), students are to discuss the two characters' different attractions towards these types of events. What do students think it is that Ben is finding from these type of events, considering his personality type and his personal character history? How does his attraction to this sub-culture and experience differ from Zoe's? Comment on how the playwright has used the element of contrast here.

HARM MINIMISATION AND DUTY OF CARE

Harm minimisation is a comprehensive approach that uses realistic strategies which must take into account three interacting components: the people involved; their social, physical and economic environment; and the drug itself.

Harm minimisation involves a range of approaches to prevent and reduce drug-related harm, including prevention, early intervention, specialist treatment, supply control, safer drug use and abstinence.

ACTIVITIES

STRATEGY BRAINSTORM AND SCRIPT ANALYSIS

... One of the most important themes in the play is the duty of care. It highlights the importance of people caring for each other and taking responsibility for each other.

Margery Forde

Brainstorm lists of activities and behaviours that students consider harmful.

Students are then to consider what things may harm others as well as themselves. For example, driving too fast could harm the driver, passengers, pedestrians and other vehicles.

Students working in small groups are to devise a series of tableaux framing some of these identified harms.

The teacher introduces and discusses the concept and approach of *Harm Minimisation and Duty of Care* to the students.

Students, working in pairs, are then to improvise Scene Seven (pgs 39–42) from the play. Following this, they are asked to identify how the concept and approach of *Harm Minimisation and Duty of Care* is being demonstrated in this scene.

Why does the playwright state that this is one of the most important themes in the play?

A sharing of responses could follow, including a brainstorm of other strategies and advice Ben could have used to ensure further minimisation of harm to his sister, Stacy, as she experimented with the drug ecstasy for the first time.

THOUGHT TRACKING

a) Students discuss the situation Ben found himself in on the night his 17-year-old sister Stacy arrived at the Crystal where she collapsed after taking a lethal drug cocktail. Students are to identify and discuss the internal conflict the character Ben may have been experiencing at the time of his sister's collapse. (The text appears in Scene Sixteen, pgs 56–58.)

b) Two students assume the roles of Stacy and Ben and the class sculpt them into position, capturing the exact moment after Stacy collapses in her brother's arms. The student enrolled as Ben then brings the scene to life using the above text and incorporating the playwright's stage directions.

c) The remaining class assume the roles of the dancers at the Crystal using stylised movement—possibly moving in slow motion.

d) All students freeze in position after Ben's final line.

e) Using the dramatic convention of 'thought tracking', the remaining class members begin to voice aloud the different thoughts that may have been going through Ben's head at this particular moment in time.

f) Students then discuss the term *Duty of Care* in response to this scene in the play. The teacher may ask students to suggest the actions Ben could have taken to help save Stacy's life.

EXTENDED ROLE PLAY FOCUSING ON DRUG USE
ISSUES: MANTLE OF THE EXPERT

a) The teacher is in the role of an anxious community leader concerned about the number of young drug-takers in his/her community. S/he seeks the help of a group of advertisers, educational psychologists, health department personnel and social workers (students in role). The community leader is concerned that current publicity, highlighting health and safety issues associated with drug use, as well as anti-drug promotion, is not really touching young people. The group lists all the skills, knowledge and understanding they possess in their expert roles and use these to design a campaign that really works. They are especially concerned with identifying why current strategies do not appear to be working. They then go on to produce the campaign, including designing a brochure for young people entitled *Duty of Care*. (Students in role should be shown samples of brochures such as *Drugs and the Law in the Sunshine State and Drugs, The Law and Young People* to help provide them with relevant resource material which will assist in informing their chosen role. Different brochures will be available in different states.) The main focus of the campaign should be the concepts of *Duty of Care* and *Harm Minimisation*. (This activity has been adapted from Jonothan Neelands' book *Structuring Drama Work*, Cambridge: University of Cambridge Press, 1990.)

b) The teacher, in role as the character Anne, goes to a teenage parent support group or her local church support group (students in role) for advice on how to deal with her teenage daughter's drug problem.

c) Students in role as school staff are gathered together to discuss the recent drug-related death of an ex-student who was expelled two years ago because she was caught smoking drugs on the school premises. The staff are also to discuss the drug problem their school continues to have and the negative profile the school is gaining as a result. They are asked to assess the seriousness of the problem and also to suggest and evaluate strategies for dealing with the problem. (Note: the school should be a fictional one as should the staff members.)

d) Students in role as parents discuss how to help and support children and teenagers 'at risk' due to drug misuse. The teacher may like to refer to points made by author Paula Goodyer in her book *Kids & Drugs* (Allen & Unwin) as a guide.

DISCUSSION: SO WHO IS RESPONSIBLE FOR STACY'S DEATH?

The teacher asks the students to generate a discussion in small groups on who they perceived or judged to be responsible for Stacy's death, using the text from the following scenes to help inform the discussion:

Scene Six, pgs 25–26
Scene Nine, pgs 35–37
Scene Ten, pgs 38–39
Scene Seventeen, pgs 58–60

WRITING IN ROLE

Students are to work in small groups and are to collectively write either:

i) The opening address of Stacy's funeral from the Priest, Father Paul, mentioning his views on drugs claiming the innocent lives of our youth.

ii) An address either Father Paul, a Drug or Alcohol Counsellor, an ex-teenage drug addict, a policeman or a social worker is invited to make at the school Stacy had attended two years prior to her death, which urges students to understand the dangers relating to illegal drug use.

iii) An address Stacy's mother, Anne, is invited to make to her local church's Sunday School, appealing to them to be aware of the dangers of drug misuse.

iv) In role as Anne, write a letter to 15-year-old Stacy trying to explain why she is upset with and disapproves of her daughter's drug behaviour.

OTHER THEMES AND ISSUES

CHOICES AND CONSEQUENCES

a) Students, working in small groups, are allocated a character from the play and are to draw up a table that contains two headings: 1) Choice, and 2) Outcome/Consequence.

b) Working in small groups, using the detailed synopsis and reflecting on their reading of the play, students are to list all of the choices their chosen character may have faced throughout their life and the outcomes/consequences that resulted.

c) Working in those same groups, students are then to represent the different choices made by the characters through a series of frozen tableaux. Each separate tableau should be given a title.

d) Students may then like to improvise different outcomes resulting from the characters choosing alternative courses of action.

ACTIVITIES EXPLORING CHARACTERS

I was putting young characters on stage and I wanted them to speak with their own voices. I didn't want to be a kind of siphon through which I would channel their thoughts and feelings. I wanted the audience to hear the voices of real young people telling things as they are.

Margery Forde

1. DISCUSSION ON THE PLAYWRIGHT'S PRTRAYAL OF CHARACTER

Playwright Margery Forde stated in a transcribed interview that her work was intensely research-based and that part of the research for *X-Stacy* involved talking to young people. Students can respond to the above quotation from the playwright, discussing her intentions when writing the play. The discussion may focus on whether or not the students felt that real young people's voices had accurately been represented through the various characters' dialogue and behaviour.

2. CHARACTER PROFILE

Select a particular point in a character's journey and create a character profile for him/her at that particular point in time. Consider the different circumstances s/he has encountered so far in the course of the action.

3. HOT-SEAT ACTIVITIES

This activity involves students being asked questions in role to which they are expected to answer spontaneously. Hot-seating can be used in various contexts to assist the students in deepening their knowledge and understanding of the different characters—their motivations, attitudes and personality. Selected students, by assuming the different characters in the play, are questioned by the remaining class group about what they think of the other characters, what they think about the events in the play, etc.

4. CHARACTER REVELATIONS

There are many revelations communicated or experienced by the characters in the play. Discuss which characters communicated or experienced the revelations, how they came to arrive at their revelation and what changes took place after the revelation occurred.

5. GENERAL FOCUS QUESTIONS ON CHARACTER DEVELOPMENT

Working in pairs, students are asked to reflect on the play, *X-Stacy*, and also to use the detailed synopsis provided at the beginning of these notes (pgs 67–70), in order to answer the following focus questions relating to a chosen character from the play:

a) How does your chosen character/s change over the course of the play? Identify the events, situations or actions of other characters that cause them to change—perhaps using a flow chart format.

b) Share the findings/discoveries with the whole class in an attempt to come to a shared understanding of both the significance of the major events that occur within the play and the effect that they have on the different characters.

6. RE-ENACTMENT OF EVENTS EXPLORING DIFFERENT CHARACTERS' POINTS OF VIEW

In small groups, students improvise the events that occurred on the night leading to Stacy's death, from the different characters' points of view; e.g., Ben, Stacy, Jenna, Fergus and Anne. The students then discuss the different interpretations.

7. UNFINISHED MATERIALS

Below is a 'created' diary entry for the character of Stacy which spans the time of the events that occur within the play.

Students are to assume the role of the character Stacy and are to complete a series of key diary entries leading up to the afternoon her mother told her to leave the house. When writing their entries, students must consider such factors as Stacy's self-esteem resulting from being expelled, her mother's disappointment in her, the loss of school friendships, isolation, idleness, etc. Students need to write a series of key entries that reflect shifting states of mind as a result of significant experiences and events.

The following is an example to provide students with a starting point:

15th October 1995

Dear Diary,

Today I got expelled from school for smoking some pot. Big deal! Well, Mum thinks it is. Shit, she went ballistic. 'Stacy, they will not have you back. You can't go back to school. Do you understand?' she says. I understand, all right. Who cares? Why on earth would I want to go back to that crap hole? What's the point? Why I was the one who got sprung is beyond me. The other guys were with me, but because Peterson couldn't see anything in their hands he couldn't spring anyone else. I was just unlucky.

The old farty arty teacher sucks. I bet he's having a session right now to help celebrate his victory. He's had it in for me for ages. Ever since I refused to hand in my art folio. 'I'm really disappointed in you, Stacy', he says. 'You have always been an exemplary student.' What if I didn't want to be an exemplary student anymore? It's my choice!

I must admit that I didn't enjoy shocking Mum like that. She doesn't deserve this type of stress. The look on her face. She was really cut. I hope she forgives me. Ben will help to convince her things are okay. He's such a cool brother. He'll be on my side.

Well, time is on my hands now. No more school, at least for now! Yeah! I'll call Jenna. She'll be rapt!

Oh, I almost forgot, today is Saint Teresa's Day.

Graciously hear us, O God our Saviour: that as we rejoice in the festival of thy blessed virgin Teresa, so we may be fed with the food of her heavenly teaching and grow in loving devotion towards thee. Through our Lord.

Stacy

A time-line of significant events has been provided below to assist with this exercise.

TIME-LINE OF SIGNIFICANT EVENTS

1980	Stacy was born.
1994	Stacy gets a toy Smurf from her brother Ben for her fourteenth birthday.
1995	Stacy gets expelled from school for smoking pot.
1996	Stacy tries 'e' for the first time and goes with her brother to a rave/dance party event.
	DJ Fergus appears at the Crystal for the first time.
1997	Stacy gets kicked out of home and dies that same night from a lethal drug cocktail.
	Jenna flees to Sydney.
1998	Nine months after Stacy's death, Jenna returns to Brisbane and meets up with a hostile Ben.

This exercise could be continued using other characters from the play:

a) Students could assume the role of JENNA and write a series of key diary entries capturing the emotional journey she experiences, beginning with the night Stacy dies and her fleeing to Sydney, until the morning after she bunks over at Ben's house with Zoe.

b) Students could assume the role of BEN and write a series of key diary entries capturing the emotional journey he experiences, beginning with the night Stacy is kicked out of home and dies, until the morning after he brings Jenna home to stay.

c) Students could assume the role of FERGUS and write a series of key diary entries capturing the emotional journey he experiences, beginning with the night Stacy dies, until the morning after his beach Rave party.

d) Students could assume the role of the priest, FATHER PAUL, and write a series of key diary entries capturing the emotional journey he experiences, beginning with the first time Anne approaches him for advice on how to handle Stacy's drug use, until the morning after Anne tells him she no longer has faith in God and His Church.

e) Students could assume the role of ZOE and write a series of diary entries capturing the emotional journey she experiences, beginning with the night she meets Ben and Fergus and moves into Anne and Ben's house, until the morning after she and Ben bring Jenna home to stay.

8. ROLE-ON-THE-WALL / CHARACTER ANALYSIS

An alternative approach to descriptive character analysis is to use the convention of role-on-the-wall. This dramatic convention involves the teacher roughly drawing a character outline of Stacy on the board. Students, working collectively as a group, add a series of statements made about Stacy by her parents, teachers, her priest, and friends. As the work progresses, new understandings about Stacy are written inside the figure as an aid to reflection and to record the growing complexity of the character.

The same convention can be used to discuss and analyse the remaining characters in the play.

A NOTE ON THE LANGUAGE OF THE PLAY

A feature of *X-Stacy* is the extensive use of strongly idiomatic language. It is language characterised by colourful imagery or by a richly idiomatic Australian or Youth slang.

The playwright has chosen not to dilute this strong language in order to make the play appear more palatable to a wider audience. Instead she has maintained its authenticity, which gives the play a strong sense of reality.

EXAMPLE 1:

> FERGUS: So, how was it?
>
> BEN: Goin' off, man. Insane stuff.
>
> FERGUS: Loony tunes.
>
> BEN: Yeah, that was a hell of a cool set. Fan-tastic.
>
> FERGUS: You've got to build a night, you know? Create a mood. Hardly anyone does that anymore. I'm trying a bit more scratching, did you notice?
>
> BEN: Nuh. [*He laughs.*] Yeah, it was bloody brilliant. It was a great night.

(Scene One, pgs 2–3)

EXAMPLE 2:

> ANNE: What's wrong?
>
> BEN: It's not like I'm sitting around on my arse all day. I'm trying to get a bloody full-time job. I've applied for three in the last fortnight.
>
> ANNE: I know you have. I wasn't having a go at you.
>
> (Scene Two, pg. 11)

Also a feature of the language is the use of swearing, particularly in the more highly-charged moments.

EXAMPLE 3:

> FERGUS *takes hold of* JENNA.
>
> FERGUS: Hey, Jenna. Cool it.
>
> JENNA: Fuck off. Ben…
>
> FERGUS: Jenna. I said cool it. Okay, babe?
>
> JENNA: Leave me alone.
>
> FERGUS: Jenna. This is really starting to piss me off.
>
> JENNA: I want to talk to Ben.
>
> FERGUS: This is not the time.
>
> JENNA: Let go. I'm talking to him.
>
> FERGUS: This is a party. Jenna? This is a party. Don't do this.
>
> JENNA: Fuck off!
>
> (Scene Fifteen, pgs 53–54)

The reason for using such language is to more accurately reflect the idiom actually spoken within youth culture. In order to maintain the credibility of the play with youth audiences it is important not to whitewash such language. Of course if it was to become over-used or used gratuitously it would weaken its impact and have the opposite effect of reducing its credibility, so the playwright is always in the situation of having to exercise careful artistic judgement.

It goes without saying that using such language can be contentious, particularly for sections of the community and for families who are committed to specific language codes that exclude the swearing idiom. No playwright wants to alienate this audience, or any other audience, but in a nation as extraordinarily diverse as ours, it can be difficult to strike a balance that neither loses its credibility for its target audience nor offends other sections of the community. Deciding where the balance lies requires a scrupulous consideration of the play's thematic and social purpose.

In this instance, the urgent need to turn the spotlight on the issue of drug use by young people makes it especially important to reflect, with honesty, the feelings, thoughts, actions and idiom of the young people most at risk. There are young people dying unnecessarily every week from drug use or abuse. Every family fears the possibility of this frightening tragedy, and so the need to confront this issue, to bring it out into the open, where it can be recognised and dealt with, drives the playwright's decision-making process when it comes to choosing the most appropriate language to help express the world of the characters.

FORUM THEATRE AND *X-STACY*

Margery Forde describes her intention in writing *X-Stacy* in this way:

[The play]... looks at the effects of a drug death on parents, and the overwhelming sense of confusion and helplessness that's felt when a child is found to be taking illegal substances. I talked to young people who take substances 'recreationally' and seem to have no problem with them. However, I talked to other young people whose lives have been almost destroyed by drugs. I also talked to their parents (including some who are my own friends) and found that there is confusion and fear when a child is found to be involved with drugs. As one mother said to me: 'I didn't know what to do. I had no road maps and neither did my son.'

I believe that through the power of theatre we can break down barriers by learning from each other's vocabularies, and experiencing each other's worlds. X-Stacy is not a critique or an explanation. It's an exploration. The play asks a lot of questions, but it doesn't always give answers. Society as a whole has to do that. But I would love to think that there would be opportunities for open and honest discussion afterwards, particularly among parents and their children. For me that would be the best possible outcome from X-Stacy.

The interactive nature of Forum Theatre seems an ideal form for stimulating the open and honest discussion that Margery Forde hopes her play will generate. Forum Theatre identifies itself as belonging to the Theatre of the Oppressed—a theatre that is about acting rather than just talking, questioning rather than giving answers, analysing rather than accepting—using theatre as a force for change.

In her play, Forde presents a variety of complex characters, all of whom are struggling to overcome their own internal oppressions. These internal oppressions and conflicts dramatically affect the way these key characters behave and the way they relate to the other characters in the play. Central to the themes of this play lie the critical issues relating to teenage drug-related death and its consequent impact on the family, the community and society as a whole. Forde states above: '*The play asks a lot of questions, but it doesn't always give answers. Society as a whole has to do that.*'

The suggested form of Forum Theatre attempts to develop the play further by *breaking down barriers*; by creating a dialogue amongst people in response to the key issues raised in the play; by attempting to train the audience (who may in some way identify with the various characters in the play or may have encountered similar situations faced by the characters) to fight against their oppressions and, in turn, empower them to begin to make steps towards resolving the conflict faced by the key character/s. This play reflects real-life issues. There are young people dying unnecessarily from drug use or abuse. Every family fears the possibility of this frightening tragedy, and so the need to confront these fears, to bring them out into the open, where they can be confronted and dealt with, is vital. Margery Forde has taken the first step in embracing this daunting challenge.

Scene Twelve (pgs 41–47) can be used as a complete model for Forum Theatre. Alternatively students might like to create the scene following Stacy being kicked out of home by her mother. Teachers may like to use this as an assessment task option which could involve students hosting and managing a Forum Theatre session where members of their local school community are invited. It should be stressed that students need to thoroughly familiarise themselves with this form of theatre before attempting it in public, and that the role of the 'joker' should be played by a mature person, possibly a teacher, as it requires the sophisticated ability to manage and facilitate without imposing any personal bias or prejudice.

GLOSSARY OF TERMS

ALTAR The table on which the sacrifice of the Mass is celebrated.

BERNINI One of the greatest Italian sculptors. His altarpiece 'The Ecstasy of St Teresa' was completed in 1645, and is displayed in the Santa Maria della Vittoria church in Rome.

BLASPHEME To swear offensively using the name of God, or Christ, or other religious terms.

CHOICE Top quality, very good.

CHILL OUT Generally means to calm down. In the Rave context a chill out room is a room where party-goers can go to in order to calm down, to withdraw from the music and to counter the dangerous effects of overheating (a side effect of taking ecstasy and then dancing for hours on end).

COMMUNION HOST/EUCHARIST The Sacrament of the Eucharist completes a person's initiation into the Christian community. In this sacrament, pieces of specially-made bread, called 'hosts' or 'communion hosts', are blessed by the priests, along with a small quantity of red wine. This is a ritual that recreates the 'last supper' when Christ had a last meal with his followers shortly before being arrested, tortured and put to death by the Roman soldiers occupying his country (Palestine, or present day Israel and Jordan). Catholics believe that when the bread and wine are blessed during the Eucharist celebration (the Mass) they become, in a mysterious way, the literal body and blood of Christ. By eating and drinking this bread and wine they become united with Christ, and with each other. Christians are not loners. They belong to a body of believers and try to live in communion with Christ and with one another. The Eucharist is the great sign of this communion.

CRUCIFIX A cross with the figure of the crucified Jesus upon it. Used by Catholics to bring to mind the sufferings of Christ.

DOOF The almost physical 'thump' of the bass line of the music played very loud at dance parties.

ECSTASY A heightened state of spiritual consciousness or awareness sometimes accompanied by euphoria. The word comes from the Greek, meaning the flight of the soul from the body.

ECSTASY A type of illegal drug often associated with Rave dance parties.

FORGIVENESS Christians (including Catholics) believe in the power of forgiveness. The central message of Christian faith is to love God and to love one another. When people do us wrong, whether deliberately or accidentally, the only way forward in a community based on love is to forgive the wrong-doer. Not to forgive, ties the soul of the injured party into bitterness and thoughts of revenge. Such thoughts poison the inner well-being of that person and compromise their ability to love. So love and forgiveness go together. But, of course, forgiveness does not come easily. It involves a process of coming to terms with the injury. Stacy's mother, Anne, and her brother, Ben, only complete this process by the end of the play and with great difficulty. Until then they are stuck in the past and cannot move forward.

We can see the same process being enacted at the national level in Australia with the Reconciliation movement, and in South Africa through the Truth and Reconciliation Commission. In both cases this involves the white communities owning up to the crimes committed against the indigenous peoples, apologising on behalf of those who committed the wrongs, and then moving forward in a spirit of openness, acceptance and generosity.

GIG A slang term very common amongst musicians, and meaning a job or a paid performance.

HARM MINIMISATION Harm minimisation is a comprehensive approach by anti-drug agencies that uses realistic strategies to minimise the harm done to people by the misuse or abuse of drugs. It takes into account three interacting components: the people involved; their social, physical and economic environment; and the drug itself.

Harm minimisation involves a range of approaches to prevent and reduce drug-related harm, including prevention, early intervention, specialist treatment, supply control, safer drug use and abstinence.

HOBBIT LAND An imaginary fantasy land created by the writer J.R. Tolkien.

LEVITATE To rise off the ground and float in the air, supposedly as a sign of being in an advanced state of spiritual development.

LIVE LIKE A PRIEST Priests in the Catholic church are not permitted to marry and must take a vow of celibacy.

MARTYR Someone who is prepared to suffer or die for their faith.

MASS The Catholic religious service. Catholics are required by their religion to attend Mass every Sunday.

MISSAL A book containing the prayers of the Mass.

PYX A special container used for transporting communion bread that has been blessed.

RAVE A particular kind of youth dance or event, often associated with drug use.

RAVE NEW WORLD A play on 'brave new world'—see *The Tempest* in the Glossary. There is a further irony. *Brave New World* was the title of Aldous Huxley's satiric novel, where he depicted a futuristic society totally controlled by drugs.

REDNECKS A term of abuse sometimes applied to ignorant, insensitive and abusive males, and sometimes to certain country people regarded as ignorant and conservative.

RELICS/HOLY RELICS Once highly valued by Christians, but much less so now, these were small items, or fragments of items, that had been used, touched or blessed by a saint (including pieces of the saint's body or clothes) that, because of their contact with the saint, reputedly had religious or healing powers. In the Middle Ages there was a great trade in these highly-prized relics, and enterprising entrepreneurs made a living selling splinters of wood and metal that supposedly came from the cross upon which Christ was crucified.

ROSARY BEADS The Rosary is a set of prayers repeated many times. To assist in counting the prayers a set of beads on a chain is used. The repetition of the prayer is an aid to concentration similar to the way that a Mantra is used in some Eastern religions. Some Catholics wear their rosary beads around their neck like a necklace.

SAINT TERESA OF AVILA A 16th-century Spanish saint, known for her mystical writings. It was reputed that she was able to enter a mystical state of ecstasy that caused her to spontaneously levitate.

SACRAMENT Special rituals or rites performed by the Church. These include Baptism (Christening) and Marriage.

SACRISTY A room in the church where the priest dresses for services and where the various sacred items (such as chalices) used in the church are kept.

SUPPLY AND DEMAND A theory of economics that says wherever there is a demand for a product or a service, there will always be a supply available, as long as the price is right. The greater the demand, then the greater the supply that will be stimulated. This is true in legal markets, but is even more the case in illegal markets such as the drug trade. As long as the demand is there, no matter what the penalties might be, the supply will always find a way through for the right money.

THE TEMPEST Shakespeare's last play, the action of which takes place on a mysterious island full of strange magic, and where the characters include a magician (Prospero), a deformed native (Caliban), and a spirit (Ariel). One of the characters describes the island as a 'Brave New World'. Prospero magically controls the actions and the characters in the play in much the same way that the DJ Fergus exerts control over Ben and Jenna. In *X-Stacy* the character Fergus dresses up as Prospero and the character Jenna as Ariel. Ariel is Prospero's servant. Prospero has promised to give Ariel his/her freedom at the end of the play's action, but, in the meantime, Ariel must perform whatever duties Prospero demands of him/her.

'TOTIN' THAT OL' CROSS' A colourful way of saying you are shouldering your burdens or fulfilling your duties no matter how heavy they might be. The image refers deliberately to Christ carrying the cross.

VIGIL A form of religious service that incorporates prayers and the action of 'keeping watch'.

ACTIVITY— MIX 'N' MATCH

Create a table from the glossary above in which terms and definitions have been deliberately mixed up. The task for the students is to match the key term with its definition or explanation. This activity would work best in small groups.

QUESTIONNAIRE

Teachers should select from these key questions to give to students in order to assist them in critiquing and evaluating the play.

EXPERIENTIAL QUESTIONS

1. Which parts of the play moved you? Why?
2. Which moments in the play have stayed with you? Why?
3. Which scenes were the most thought-provoking? Why?
4. Which scenes did not work for you? Why?
5. Which parts of the play amused you? Why?
6. Which characters could you especially relate to? Why?
7. Which characters could you not relate to? Why?
8. Were there any parts of the play that shocked you? Why?
9. Were there any parts of the play that made you feel uncomfortable? Why?
10. How does this play differ from other plays you have read?

PRODUCTION ELEMENTS

1. How could the costumes and general appearance of the actors contribute to your understanding of the characters?
2. How could lighting and sound contribute to the overall meaning and effect of the play?
3. How could technical or design elements be used to help create a variety of moods?
4. How could you make the shifts in time between past and present clear? Consider lighting, sound, direction, acting, etc.
5. Comment on the characterisation. Are the characters believable? How could actors capture the teenage characters on stage?
6. How could actors use gesture, pace and vocal tone to convey their characters to the audience?
7. What is the purpose and effect of the same actor doubling the roles of the Priest and Fergus?
8. *X-Stacy* has many scene changes, requiring quick changes in place, time and mood. How could the show's design—set, costume, lighting and sound—assist in keeping the action moving?

STYLE

1. Comment on the style of the play. What makes it innovative in its form?
2. What makes this play distinctly Australian?
3. *X-Stacy* could be described as being '*a very demanding piece of theatre*'. Do you agree? Why? Why not?

EVALUATION

1. Is this a play anyone could read and enjoy? If yes, why? If not, why not?
2. How effectively did the production capture:
   parent/teenage relationships
   rave and dance party culture
   issues of Australian concern
   drug culture
   moral and religious issues
   grief
   youth culture
   resolution/reconciliation
   blame and forgiveness
   choice and responsibility
   the challenges of parenting
   the implications of trust and loyalty
   male/female relationships?

3. Margery Forde, in a transcribed interview, says that: '*I believe that the writer's role in society is to show the world on the stage, to hold a mirror up to us so we can learn about ourselves and each other.*' What did you personally learn from reading *X-Stacy*? What thoughts remained with you afterwards?

*****

HELEN RADVAN graduated from the Queensland University of Technology in 1989 with a Diploma in Teaching. In the last ten years she has completed her Bachelor of Education and has worked as a Drama Teacher with Education Queensland, and as a Part-time Lecturer in the Drama Department at the Queensland University of Technology. She has written a series of Teacher's Notes for both La Boite Theatre and QUT.

RESOURCE MATERIAL, SUPPORT SERVICES AND AGENCIES

RESOURCES AND PUBLICATIONS

Drug Education: Do it. Commonwealth Department of Human Services and Health, 1996.

This *Drug Education: Do it* series has been produced by the Drugs of Dependence Branch as part of the Commonwealth National Initiatives in Drug Education (NIDE) project. The documents offer guidelines:

• for the development of drug education curriculum within a health education program;
• to enable schools and agencies to work more effectively together to provide drug education for students;
• for the design of pre-service and in-service training through the identification of competencies for teachers of drug education; and
• for the selection of drug education resources in schools.

ADIS
The Alcohol and Drug Information Service
operates 24 hours a day, 7 days a week
Telephone: (07) 3236 2414
Country areas (toll free) 1800 177 833

AA (ALCOHOLICS ANONYMOUS)
A self-help organisation for people with alcohol problems. Groups meet throughout each State.
Telephone (07) 3255 9162

CEIDA
Centre for Education & Information on Drugs and Alcohol,
The Langton Centre,
Cnr. Nobbs and South Dowling Streets,
Surry Hills, NSW, 2010.
Telephone (02) 9331 2196

DRUG ARM
Drug and Alcohol Crisis Line
Telephone (07) 3368 3822

COMMUNITY HEALTH CENTRES
In many areas, these centres employ specialist drug and alcohol workers. They can help with information, advice and referral. Look in your phone book under Department of Health.

QUEENSLAND HEALTH
Alcohol, Tobacco and Other Drugs Branch
Telephone: (07) 3328 9833

Direct contact with someone who has been involved in the writing and development of the play is Mr Benjamin Norris (Social Worker), Senior Project Officer, *Alcohol, Tobacco and Other Drugs* Branch
Telephone: (07) 3234 1942

COMMUNITY SOLUTIONS
This organisation works in association with Queensland Health.
Telephone: (07) 5413 1555

TEEN CHALLENGE
PO Box 3376
South Brisbane Qld 4101
Phone: (07) 3422 1500